Ple𝚊
Dychwelw

D1486406

AGAINST THE ODDS

AGAINST
THE
ODDS

President Goodluck Jonathan, the Rise of
Nigeria as Africa's Economic Superpower
and the threat of Boko Haram

Copyright © 2015 Susquehanna Press, 2015

The moral right of the author has been asserted.

Apart from any fair dealing for the purposes of research or private study,
or criticism or review, as permitted under the Copyright, Designs and Patents
Act 1988, this publication may only be reproduced, stored or transmitted, in
any form or by any means, with the prior permission in writing of the
publishers, or in the case of reprographic reproduction in accordance with
the terms of licences issued by the Copyright Licensing Agency. Enquiries
concerning reproduction outside those terms should be sent to the publishers.

Matador
9 Priory Business Park
Kibworth Beauchamp
Leicestershire LE8 0RX, UK
Tel: (+44) 116 279 2299
Fax: (+44) 116 279 2277
Email: books@troubador.co.uk
Web: www.troubador.co.uk/matador

ISBN 978 1784621 339

British Library Cataloguing in Publication Data.
A catalogue record for this book is available from the British Library.

Typeset in 11pt Adobe Garamond Pro by Troubador Publishing Ltd
Printed and bound in the UK by TJ International, Padstow, Cornwall

Matador is an imprint of Troubador Publishing Ltd

Susquehanna Press is a new company
devoted to publishing books mainly on Africa

CONTENTS

PROLOGUE

Just before midnight on April 14, 2014, a group of self-styled Islamist militants known as Boko Haram and disguised as Nigerian soldiers kidnapped 267 female high school students in Chibok, Borno State, in the North-East region of the country.

The terrorists had arrived in large convoys dressed in army uniforms and their cars painted in military colours. Earlier that night they had detonated some explosives outside of the town, close enough for the young girls and their teachers to hear the bombs and the commotion. Then they drove up to the school and told the girls that they were there to save them from Boko Haram who was attacking. "They looked exactly like the military and the girls had heard the explosions, so that's why they went with them voluntarily, because they thought they were going to safety", said Fatima Akilu, a Director at Nigeria's National Security Council. "That was why they were able to round them up so quickly, and to kidnap so many. The girls that escaped told us later that they didn't realise it wasn't the military until they had been driven into the forest. There, at one point, the car broke down and they managed to escape".

Earlier that day, a massive explosion at a bus station packed with morning commuters at Nyanya, on the outskirts of the capital Abuja, killed at least 88 people and injured another 125. It was Boko Haram's most deadly and devastating attack to date on the capital. Witnesses described a man parking a car near a police checkpoint next to the bus station. The man walked away and within a few seconds the car blew up. The incident immediately raised fears that the Islamic militants were trying to expand their area of operation. Before this bombing, there had not been a terrorist attack in the capital for over two years. In a chilling video message posted on Youtube soon after the atrocity, a Boko Haram leader calling himself "Abubakar Shekau", said: "We are in your city but you don't know where we are."

The timing of the blast at the bus top in Nyanya was a clever, if not especially original, military tactic. For it diverted resources away from the hunt for the kidnapped girls further north and stretched the capacity of security agencies to the limit. For a short period it overshadowed the crisis in Chibok. In fact, the abduction of the pupils was just the latest in a series of increasingly brutal attacks against schools in the North East which prompted the Jonathan administration to close down all schools in the region on a temporary basis – advice that the Borno State Government chose to ignore. Three months earlier, Boko Haram militants barricaded the doors to a boys' dormitory of the College of Buni Yadi, a secondary school near Damaturu, Yobe State, and set the building on fire, killing 59 by burning them alive. The death of those boys, however, never made the headlines. Nor, at first, did the events in Chibok. It was regarded as just another phase in the gruesome saga of one of Africa's forgotten insurgencies.

But then Social Media intervened and momentum gathered around the fate of the kidnapped children. A twitter campaign #bringbackourgirls attracted large numbers of followers, including Michelle Obama and Angelina Jolie. There were demonstrations in cities throughout the US and Europe. By early May 2014, world leaders began to show interest and demanded action. And at home in Nigeria prominent opposition members were demonstrating on the streets, carrying banderols with the same slogan. But by August 2014, only 57 of the girls had managed to escape and it was clear that this was no ordinary abduction.

There are many factors that made Chibok unusual and distinctive: the sheer audacity of kidnapping so many girls at once was just one. But the absence of a ransom demand was the most striking. Contrary to their normal practice, Boko Haram never demanded money or explained what they wanted in exchange for the release of the girls. "I remember thinking that there must soon come a demand or a ransom, because there must be a reason why they would take such a large number", said Akilu. "It was a tragedy for the girls who were just about to sit their exams, go to university and prepare for the next stage of their lives. There were rumours of a ransom and we heard about it from our people on the ground in Maiduguri. But no one ever stepped forward. I just don't know why they never just came out with their demands".

The kidnapping was a costly operation, and without the

potential reward of a ransom payment, why were these young militants living in the Sambisa forest willing to expend resources on such an attack? The tactical sophistication and planning required to co-ordinate the kidnapping and the bombing was far beyond anything that had been seen by the Boko Haram to that date.

Many observers believed that the answer lay in the fact that Nigeria was preparing to host the World Economic Forum just three weeks later on May 8 2014. The showcase of this prestigious summit of political and business leaders was how African countries were generating high economic growth, reflecting a new dynamism that was pulling the continent out of poverty and backwardness. And Nigeria, the largest market on the continent, was held up as the shining star of the new rising Africa. A revision and reinterpretation of GDP data in April 2014 suggested that Nigeria's economy was nearly 90 per cent larger than had previously been estimated, surpassing South Africa as the largest economy on the continent, and that growth in 2014 was an estimated eight per cent.

The conference was designed to be a defining moment in the Presidency of Goodluck Jonathan, a mild-mannered former academic who was introducing new reforms in an attempt to reduce corruption and modernize the economy. Against the odds, Nigeria appeared to be at last fulfilling its promise. Military dictatorship was becoming a distant memory. But the positive economic news was drowned out by the media firestorm generated by the terrorist attacks and the global clamour to #bringbackourgirls. Abuja was turned into a city under siege with roadblocks and security checkpoints that choked traffic as the government sought to reassure heads of states and dignitaries of their security.

The sense that Boko Haram was targeting the conference was compounded by the fact that a ransom had still not been demanded. And then on 1 May, one week before the summit, Abuja was hit again when a second blast in Nyanya killed another 20 people. The timing of the terrorist acts, especially the targeting of Abuja, partially succeeded in silencing the news of the promising economic statistics. Instead of celebration, the Jonathan government was criticised for inadequate security and not dealing with terrorism.

For Boko Haram the timing was immaculate and they were not shy in using video rollouts and manipulating social and international media to promote their message. Nigerian specialists are convinced that both the kidnapping and the two bombings were politically motivated. It was not Jihad. "This is not about Islam", said Dr Stephen Davis, an advisor to two former Presidents who for three months conducted his own independent mediation with the Boko Haram to free the girls. "This is about terrorising the public. This is about political sponsors (donors) wanting to take over the government in Nigeria. It is about greed and power, that's what it is all about."

Based on intensive and extensive interviews throughout the country, including meetings with operatives and religious figures close to the insurgents, Dr Davis' investigation was startling and explosive. He concluded that Boko Haram was being secretly funded and armed by some Nigerian politicians in the northern region from both the ruling People's Democratic Party and the opposition All Progressive's Congress who he refers to as the "political sponsors". Their aim, he said, was to create chaos in order to discredit President Jonathan and cast him as unfit to rule. It was a silent coup.

Critics countered by asking why the Jonathan administration has not arrested these politicians who have clearly committed the most serious crimes imaginable – financing mass murder of innocent people and high treason. "So why didn't the President just go and grab these guys?", replied Dr Davis. "Well, could you imagine the domestic and international outcry if the President arrested prominent politicians who also happen to be members of the opposition party? The world would say 'Oh, here we go again, this is Nigeria. He is trying to nobble the elections by taking out the opposition.'"

At first Dr Davis thought that there was a very good chance of rescuing the captured girls or negotiating their freedom. But he was constantly frustrated that his operation was impeded until it dawned on him that the release of the girls was linked to the elections due in February 2015. He believes that some politicians do not want the kidnapped children to be released before the election. "It is very clear to me now that getting the girls back is just a sideshow", said Davis. "The only way to stop this from happening again is to take out the political sponsors."

The kidnapping crisis catapulted President Jonathan into the international media spotlight. It came as a challenge for the diffident, introverted politician, a leader who never expected to be President. Who exactly was this reflective, softly spoken man who was in stark contrast to his macho bellicose predecessors? And how had he risen so meteorically through the ranks to become President? Those advisors close to Jonathan talk of a circumspect thoughtful politician who believes in long-term solutions and has been underestimated at every turn.

In the overheated atmosphere surrounding the kidnapping of the girls, it became difficult to see the quieter, subtler strategy being implemented. In that sense, Boko Haram and its sponsors have been winning the propaganda war based on adept manipulation of social and international media. But Jonathan has been blessed with good luck and his country has made remarkable progress in the past decade.

Today Nigeria is the world's largest black nation. One out of five Africans lives there. It is the only sub-Saharan African country to be rated among the world's leading emerging economies and its youthful demographics and high growth rates point to a growing middle class over the next decade. It is a dynamic, challenging country, still burdened by its past but increasingly reaching out to a more hopeful and prosperous future. Its approximately 170-million people are roughly equally divided between Christian and Muslim, who have been living together in relatively mutual tolerance that, before the rise of Boko Haram, demonstrated that people of such different faiths could co-exist.

President Jonathan has ambitious plans to eradicate corruption, open up the energy sector, restore the country's farming system, reform state-owned industries and provide schooling to millions of children. Much has been achieved over the last five years, despite the terrorist threat of Boko Haram. The challenge now is to implement this brave new world. If he is successful, then it could be a landmark for the whole of Africa.

Chapter One

A RELUCTANT POLITICIAN

President Goodluck Jonathan's entry into politics was actually expedited by a judge, not a politician. In Jonathan's home state of Bayelsa, few people had more influence than Justice Igoniwari who was regarded as a father figure in the area. And so in 1998 when Chief D. S. P. Alamieyeseigha (pronounced al-ah-mess-ee-ya) was looking for a deputy as his running mate for Governor when Nigeria prepared for the return to civilian rule, he consulted the influential Judge, a former politician himself. Justice Igoniwari recommended Jonathan after listening to his thoughtful contributions at political meetings. "I prayed over it because I never wanted a deputy that would give me problem," recalled Alamieyeseigha. "I presented the matter to God and so when Justice Igoniwari recommended him, it clicked as if my eyes were open."

The following week Alamieyeseigha drove to Jonathan's modest house in Port Harcourt with veteran politician and business leader Gordon Bozimo. Alamieyeseigha asked whether Jonathan would run as his deputy for the Governorship. They did not know each other and had never met before. At first Jonathan refused. It was only when former Governor of Rivers State Chief Melford Okilo, of the Ogbia

Brotherhood, and local elders spoke to Jonathan that he relented and agreed. It was his regional origins that made the difference. In Nigerian politics block voting is a powerful force. Alamieyeseigha, a retired Air Force officer, knew that if he chose a candidate from the Ogbia electorate as his deputy for the race then he could count on Jonathan to deliver the whole district.

Despite some last-minute reticence, Jonathan resigned from his job as environment director of the Oil and Mineral Producing Areas Development Commission, an agency set up in 1992 to help develop the Niger Delta, and the campaign was on. "I had no problem with him accepting but when you are in a place receiving your daily bread and somebody says you should resign and come to an area that you are not even sure about, it was not so easy," recalled Alamieyeseigha.

Jonathan's reluctance to enter the political arena is reflected by the fact that before the approach from Alamieyeseigha he betrayed no signs of political ambition. His origins are very humble and attending secondary school was considered a luxury, and a political career was never even spoken of. Goodluck Ebele Jonathan was born on November 20, 1957, in Otouke, within the Ogbia Kingdom, in the Eastern Region, which is now Bayelsa State. It is the smallest state in Nigeria, with an estimated population of just over 1.5 million.

Otouke is a mere 20 minutes drive from the first commercial oil well found in Nigeria. When Jonathan was born, there were no proper roads in Bayelsa. To travel from

Otouke to Port Harcourt would take an entire day – which would have seemed like a lifetime and a world away for any young boy like Jonathan. In fact, he did not even hear the sound of a car until he was six years old when a Shell Land Rover was travelling on the dirt road between his village and a neighbouring one. He immediately ran into the bush in fear. "In my early days in school I had no shoes, no school bags", recalled Jonathan. "I carried my books in my hands but never despaired. There was no car to take me to school, but I never despaired. There were days I had only one meal, but I never despaired. I walked miles and crossed rivers to school every day, but I never despaired. [I] didn't have power, didn't have generators, studied with lanterns, but I never despaired."

Commentators have reflected on Jonathan's unusual name. But many Nigerians believe one's name can help shape a person's destiny. So they tend to bestow on their children names with significant meaning. It is not uncommon to meet people named Fortune, Happiness, Charity, or God's Gift. Names given in their native language are also imbued with symbolic and often religious meaning. Jonathan's middle name Ebele (or Ebelemi) means "God's wish." His late father, Lawrence, said that he "called him Goodluck because although life was hard for me when he was born, I had this feeling that this boy would bring me good luck."

Jonathan is a Christian from the Ijaw tribe and was brought up speaking the local language of Ogbia. He was raised in a Niger Delta, in a polygamous family of canoe makers. His paternal grandmother, Sara, named him "Azikiwe" after Dr Nnamdi Azikiwe, a former Nigerian nationalist leader who went on to become Nigeria's first President – a rather controversial name during the Nigerian civil war that raged in the late 1960s, with the oil fields of the Niger Delta a key prize for both federal forces and Biafran secessionists.

Jonathan was the third of nine children, of which only he and his elder sister Obebatien survived. His mother, Eunice, moved out of the family home after his father married his second wife in 1960. There are no records of Eunice ever remarrying.

Jonathan attended St. Stephens (now State School Otuoke) and St. Michael's (Oloibiri) Primary Schools. In 1971, aged 14, he proceeded to Mater Dei High School, Imiringi, where he received his West African School Certificate in 1975 ("Passed with Distinctions"). All three schools were run by the Church and located in his home state.

When asked by the authors to recite a vivid memory from his childhood Jonathan laughs and answers:

"Well I grew up in a very rural area. And when you grow up in such a simple way there are so many memories. There is so much to do. I don't know if any of them is extraordinary in any way, particularly exciting for you, but for me, I have many vivid memories. There were also many challenges of course.

"I remember when I was moving from primary school to secondary school. I was very interested in school. I left primary school in 1969. Then my father was a bit reluctant, not that he did not support me, no, but he was worried how he was going to cope.

"Back then, and especially where I grew up, going to secondary school was a very big thing, not everyone did. No, only a few were fortunate. In the rural setting the schools were very far and you were expected to pay some money so many people just felt like they were not going to cope.

"So you see my father was a bit reluctant, so I missed that first year of school because he did not know how he was going to cope. But we did, so it was in the second year that I began secondary school. I was one year late but I remember the excitement I felt when I could continue, to move to another level of education, it was so big, it brought me so much excitement. I was only a young boy but now people looked at me differently. I was now someone who was in secondary school, I was given that respect. I felt so proud.

"I am not sure this is a vivid memory that you were thinking, I am not sure whether it is very exciting, but I remember I was very proud."

After graduating from high school, Jonathan worked with the Customs and Excise Department as a Preventive Officer until 1977, when he gained admission into the University of Port Harcourt. He graduated in 1981 with a BSc in Zoology and later obtained an MSc in Hydrology and Fisheries Biology and a doctorate in Zoology. He later worked as an Inspector of Science Education, and at the Rivers State College of Education as a Lecturer. In 1993, he was appointed Assistant Director (Ecology) of the now-defunct Oil Mineral Producing Area Development Commission (OMPADEC) in charge of Environmental Protection.

It was from this rarefied, academic and technical world

that Jonathan entered the hectic atmosphere of Nigerian politics in 1998. But having no political baggage was in one sense an asset and he used this to his advantage when he ran with Alamieyeseigha against Doukpolagha, who was the candidate for Governor for the All Nigeria Peoples Party (ANPP), a legacy of the All Progressives Congress (APC).

Doukpolagha, a retired accountant and banker, was a credible candidate with a relatively clean history. However, as is often the case in Nigeria, the elections were not won by policy manifestos, but by strategic alliances. Since its formation in 1998 the strength of the PDP has been its wide membership base, with a breadth of people from all across the country, from North to South. By knitting together a strategic network of powerful people with a populist base, PDP targeted almost everyone on the electoral list of voters.

Within Bayelsa, Alamieyeseigha and Jonathan together covered far more ground than Doukbolagha and his team could have dreamt of. On the national stage, the PDP also had a greater reach, stronger networks and better funding. The party went into the 1999 elections with the momentum as front-runner, and has dominated Nigeria's political space ever since.

Nigeria's political and business culture likes winners, and likes certainties. This creates huge challenges for any opposition parties and leaders, beset by internal divisions, institutional weakness and a widely held perception that opposition parties are either regional shows or homes for the disaffected or those cast off by the PDP.

For example, Atiku Abubakar, the former vice-President (1999-2007), who helped found the PDP in 1998, decided to leave the party and stand against it when he found his ambitions blocked by President Obasanjo, who had been reluctantly forced to contemplate his departure from office at the end of his constitutionally mandated second, four-year term in 2007.

Atiku rejoined the PDP to challenge the leadership again before the 2011 elections, only to lose out and ultimately leave the party again in 2013 for the seemingly more promising pastures of the opposition he had already also once abandoned.

Similarly, Muhammadu Buhari, a former military ruler (1983-95) from Katsina in the far North, took a flexible approach to the pursuit of power: he stood for the ANPP against Obasanjo in 2003 and again against Yar'Adua in 2007, before setting up his own party which in turn has now merged back with the ANPP and other regional parties and splinter factions to form an uneasy broad church marked by self-interest and ambition. If Buhari runs again in the upcoming 2015 election, it shall be his fourth attempt at the presidency.

Jonathan's political education has been very different, characterised by little of the sharp-elbowed ruthlessness for which Nigeria's typically adversarial politics is so notorious. Early in his political career Jonathan realised that he needed to build alliances with people from across the country, including the north; to make concessions to reach a consensus; to work within and help promote strong institutions independent from manipulation by individuals; and to submit to due and proper process.

Jonathan served as Deputy Governor from May 29, 1999, to December 12, 2005. He had an amicable relationship with Alamieyeseigha, but they were never close or even political associates. Jonathan was not considered important enough by the Alamieyeseigha administration and was therefore not particularly well treated. Indeed, there were other people, closer to the Governor, who were more powerful and Jonathan was regarded as a mere figurehead. One of Jonathan's political associates from that era agreed: "As a Vice President in Nigeria you still have some duties awarded to you by the constitution. But as a Deputy Governor you have nothing. This is not just in Bayelsa, but across the country. Deputy Governors are disposable. It is the Governor that decides everything."

Known as "Alams", Alamieyeseigh and his aides treated Jonathan with arrogant, almost lofty, disdain, and instead deferred to the Governor's "Man Friday", Ebifemowei, his cousin who became his *de facto* deputy Governor.[1] Ebifemowei was officially the "Transport Officer", in charge of co-ordinating the Governor's motorcade. But behind the scenes he was Alamieyeseigha's right hand, and in charge of large budgets.

Today, ten years later, Alamieyeseigha tells a very different story:[2] "My working relationship with Dr Goodluck Jonathan was not a master-subordinate relationship. I took him as a younger brother and he accepted me as his elder brother, so everything went smoothly. I don't have to think twice before traveling because I know that my younger brother effectively manages the state till I come back. Even with our wives, he calls my wife mummy and my wife takes him as a son. My wife prefers to deal with him on official matters than me because I am the hard type, very hard. So till today, I take Patience as my daughter and that is how she accepts me too."

But according to a close aide of the President, who has worked alongside Jonathan since his time as Deputy Governor, this is nothing but a clever and amusing rewriting of history. "Of course he and Goodluck were like brothers," laughed the aide. "Now he says this! I mean who would not want to be brothers with a President? Let's just say it is more of a retrospective brotherhood. Back then he would not give Jonathan an inch. He hardly ever spoke to him. Ebifemowei, his cousin, was very much his second in command, not Jonathan."

Such treatment exasperated Jonathan. He was so frustrated that late one night in 2005 Jonathan went to see a family friend at night and virtually begged him to help him ask an elder statesman to appeal to Alams, on his behalf, to put an end to the charade and his unfair treatment. Despite his alienation, Jonathan, a former teacher, devoted his time as deputy governor to education reform. "Education was so key to him", said Jonathan's aide. "It would always be close to his heart".

He implemented a policy that enabled the best performing students from the rural primary schools across the state to receive grants and continue their education at the elite institutions in Lagos. As a result, children who had never even been to Yenagoa – the state capital of Bayelsa – were now being sent to the best schools in Lagos alongside the children of the elite.

As Deputy Governor and Governor Jonathan received numerous awards for his diplomatic and conciliatory style. He was voted the "Best Performing Deputy Governor" in 2002 by the Institute of Public Analysts of Nigeria (IPAN). He was also given the "Democracy and Good Governance Award" by Nigeria Union of Journalists in 2004. The Nigerian Union of Teachers then voted him the "Best Performing Governor in Education in the South-South" in 2006. That same year he was also recognized by the International Federation for World Peace (IIFWP), with the "Ambassador for Peace Merit Award", as well as the "Leadership and Good Governance Merit Award". The Africa International News magazine honoured him with the "Niger Delta Development Award", and he was also given the "Africa Leadership Award" by the All African Students Union in South Africa, also in 2006.

In stark contrast, Alamieyeseigha was a combative and outspoken politician, who led a vociferous campaign against the government's federal control of the state's oil funds, pushing for greater budgetary control to remain within the state. As a result, Alamieyeseigha made political enemies in Abuja, including President Obasanjo, who suspected he was one of the players opposing his plans to change the constitution to stay on indefinitely in office. When Alamieyeseigha was accused of mismanagement of Bayelsa state funds the authorities did not hesitate to move against him.

On September 15, 2005, Alamieyeseigha was detained at Heathrow airport in London and had his passport confiscated. He faced three different money-laundering charges after the Metropolitan police found over £1 million in cash in his London home, another £1.8 million in various bank accounts, and traced London real estate worth an estimated £10 million. His next court hearing was scheduled for December 8, but Alamieyeseigha jumped his £1.25 million bail bond and instead showed up in Yenagoa, the capital of Bayelsa state, on November 20, 2005.

The tale of how the Governor escaped British jurisdiction has elements of slapstick that could have been borrowed from a movie starring the Marx Brothers or Laurel and Hardy. According to one widely reported version, dressed as a woman, Alamieyesiegha took a Eurostar train from London to Paris and then flew to Douala, a port city in Cameroon neighbouring Nigeria, where a speedboat took him home under the cover of darkness. His subterfuge was helped by the fact that he had lost weight during his stay in Europe, which included a visit to a German clinic for cosmetic surgery to reduce the fat around his stomach.

When asked by reporters how he evaded British controls to make it back to Bayelsa, Alamieyeseigha, denied the cross-dressing speculation, but was coy and initially said, "I don't know myself. I just woke up and found myself in Amassoma [Bayelsa's third city]." Nuhu Ribadu, the Chairman of Nigeria's anti-corruption body the Economic and Financial Crimes Commission (EFCC), later said that Alamieyeseigha had "forged documents" to enable his flight from justice.

Naturally, the media had a field day with his exploits. Alamieyeseigha was dubbed a "Master of Deception" by *ThisDay* newspaper, which published a digital photomontage of him in a red dress, matching headpiece, sparkling necklace and lipstick. And there were soon calls for him to resign as Bayelsa's governor. The speaker of the State House of Assembly, Rt. Hon. Peremobowei Ebebi, said: "A governor who disguised himself as a woman to run away from justice in London should not be our governor. It is slap on our collective dignity as a people and our sensibilities as a people."

In the face of such lurid and compromising detail, Alamieyeseigha adopted a policy of stout denial. In a lively account he gave to the media in 2010, he pronounced himself innocent of all charges. The way Alams tells it he had travelled to Europe to undergo a "major surgical operation" in Germany, which involved him being on the operating table for eight hours.

Fifteen days later, having had his stitches removed, he flew to London with his children. It was when that flight landed at Heathrow that his troubles began. The plane was boarded by officers of London's Metropolitan Police who, after confirming his identity, announced that they were arresting him for money-laundering.

Alamieyeseigha takes up the story: "I said, 'No, you cannot arrest me. By international law, I am not even in your territory yet. I am still in the aircraft and had not even passed immigration. Secondly, I am an executive governor of a state in Nigeria.' I claimed my sovereign immunity. Detective Sergeant Ingram of the Metropolitan Police said to me 'You have no immunity. Your president said he has waived your immunity and we should arrest you.' And I asked, 'My president said so'? He responded in the affirmative. I asked him, 'Can you arrest any governor from any of the states in America if they commit offence here in your territory?' He said, 'No, but your president said we should arrest you.' He then put a call to Obasanjo and put the phone on speaker, and said: 'Mr President sir, the subject, the Governor of Bayelsa State, has been arrested. He is with us.' Then Obasanjo blurted out: 'Hold him o, hold him o, hold him o'. When I heard his voice, my spirit became dampened and then he used the other phone to call the Inspector General of Police [in Nigeria] to say that my people will react, so they should send mobile policemen from Port Harcourt and Delta to Bayelsa State."

The police then searched Alamieyeseigha and his children before putting him in handcuffs. By this time, according to the Governor, his surgical wounds had started to bleed to the extent that his clothes were "soaked with blood". At this point "the police took pity on me" and removed the handcuffs before leading the family off the aircraft. Once inside the terminal Alamieyeseigha was formally identified by Nuhu Ribadu of the EFCC before being taken into custody.

The next morning, Alamieyeseigha hired a lawyer, a fellow Nigerian called Odita, who suggested they attempt to vacate some of the bail conditions. "We did not even spend three minutes in court," claimed Alamieyeseigha. "I was discharged and acquitted because they had nothing. As I was going home, I was rearrested by the same people and was taken back to detention. The following day, I was taken to a magistrate court on three charges. One, that in year 2000, somebody gave me £475,000. The second charge was that in 2003, another person gave me £400-and-something thousand and that it passed through me to somebody. The third charge was that they found money in my house approximately a million pounds in different currencies."

"Those were the three very frivolous charges and they took me to a racist court. My lawyer was not even allowed to talk. I was just remanded in prison custody and they took me to Brixton Prison and kept me with mad people. I was with mad people for 15 days. Eventually good Samaritans rallied round and tried to get me bailed. Anybody that came up to be one of the sureties was in trouble. The person's account will be frozen and will be investigated. It was terrible."

Alamieyeseigha gives a very different version of the chain of events that followed once he was out on bail. The way he tells it, there was no dressing up as a woman to take the Eurostar. Instead he makes the improbable claim that the British authorities flew him to Cote d'Ivoire where he had the good fortune to meet a friendly fellow countryman:

"I was lucky a Nigerian was coming to do business in a chartered aircraft because I had no passport," he said. "I was just stranded in Ivory Coast in the evening when this Good Samaritan saw me. He was excited and asked what I was doing in Ivory Coast and I narrated my ordeal. So he said I should join him and he brought me back to Nigeria. I got home late. We flew to Lagos and the same aircraft took me to Port Harcourt. It was in Lagos I called my ADC to come and pick me at the airport and that was how I got home. I never dressed like a woman to escape from London. There were a lot of things and I am only abridging it because the stories are highly classified. The only thing I can say is that it is unfortunate."

Given that Alamieyeseigha had been accused of robbing blind his own people, it seems fair to assume that he would have tried to keep his return as low key as possible. Far from it, he returned to the Governor's mansion on November 22 2005, where he was treated to a hero's welcome. Crowds assembled outside cheered and waved tree branches and palm fronds. Addressing his supporters, Alamieyeseigha said: "I cannot tell you how I was brought here. It is a mystery. All the glory goes to God. Today I am back at my desk, forever committed to serve the people of Bayelsa and Nigeria. I thank the almighty God for his protection."

There was no divine intervention when it came to the machinery of justice, however. Alamieyeseigha was duly charged with money laundering, which then lead to his impeachment and prosecution. As his deputy, Jonathan was in line to assume the Governorship but he initially "refused to take over," according to the human rights attorney Oronto Douglas – like both Alamieyeseigha and Jonathan an Ijaw. "Jonathan said the rule of law must take its course." As a result, associates of Alamieyeseigha kept their hold on power, even when the Governor was under house arrest. It was only when the situation reached a point where Jonathan was constitutionally obliged to take over that he reluctantly assumed the Governorship. To some, Jonathan's behaviour may appear excessively cautious, but his insistence on doing things by the book has repeatedly stood him in good stead: he owed his position to letter and spirit of the law, rather than the web of obligations to power brokers and barons so typically at the centre of a Nigerian's politician's career.

Alamieyeseigha's supporters claimed, and still maintain, that the charges against him were "politically motivated". To this day Alamieyeseigha remains a very popular politician in his home state, and his supporters believe that the anti-corruption drive against him was part of a wider campaign to target Obasanjo's political opponents. It is true that the federal government considered him something of an irritant because of his demands for more control over the Niger Delta's mineral resources. While there seems little doubt that Alamieyeseigha illegally siphoned off state funds he was by no means alone in doing this and many believe that he was singled out for confronting Obasanjo. Such was the level of support for him locally that his impeachment was carried out only after members of the Bayelsa State House of Assembly were detained by the EFCC in Lagos and returned under heavy guard to Yenagoa to vote for his removal in return for their freedom.

Some critics believe that Jonathan should have stepped aside as well on the grounds that he must have been aware of what Alamieyeseigha's was up to. No paper trails connected Jonathan to any of Alamieyeseigha's dealings, however, and no witnesses came forward to implicate him. As a result, he was not mentioned in Ribadu's report on the affair. Jonathan's allies, both today and at the time he was Deputy Governor, believe he was kept well out of it perhaps because Alamieyeseighaga had no desire to share his booty, or – if he did – it would have been with his cousin the "Transport Officer". The consensus is that Alamieyeseigha and Jonathan were nothing but a convenient alliance. Jonathan was given the task of sorting out education and it was made clear to him that he wasn't expected to concern himself with other matters. This was a request with which he had few options other than to comply.

"A Nigerian Governor once described Deputy Governors as mere spare tyres," said a close aide to Jonathan. "Most Governors, including Alamieyeseigha, kept their Deputies well outside the loop, and actively worked to diminish their influence because they feared them as potential usurpers. Jonathan was definitely not in the loop in what was happening in the Alamieyesigha's government."

Eventually Alamieyeseigha became the first ex-Governor to plead guilty to corruption charges in Nigeria but his conviction did not stand for long. On 12 March, 2013, he was pardoned by Jonathan, a move which was heavily criticised by the media as a "political stunt". The truth is that Jonathan was in a difficult position. At the time he was campaigning for re-election against a background of insurgency in the North, opposition from a range of political heavyweights and – above all – a very fragile peace in the Niger Delta.

In such a context, the idea of going into an election with Alamieyeseigha, the self-appointed "Governor-General of the

Ijaw Nation", stirring up trouble in his own back yard was not an attractive one to Jonathan. Far better to secure his support via a pardon.

Jonathan's allies point out that Machiavellian deals of this sort are struck all over the world, citing President Clinton's infamous pardoning of Marc Rich. The billionaire financier and oil trader was a generous donor to Clinton's Democratic Party. But after being indicted on 65 criminal counts, including racketeering and tax evasion, he became a fugitive. In one of his last acts as president Clinton granted him a pardon, sparking a storm of protest in response.

Jonathan had not been Governor for long when he was again summoned by the PDP establishment. Following Obasanjo's eight-year reign, the party had "agreed" on a Muslim northerner, Umaru Musa Yar'Adua, as its next Presidential candidate. However, escalating chaos and community anger in the Niger Delta had prompted calls for the Vice President to be picked from the troubled region. Ironically, this was another position that Jonathan gained thanks to the front runner being ruled out by corruption allegations. The Governor of the oil-rich Rivers State, Dr. Peter Otunuya Odili, had been the first choice of the party hierarchy and was favourite to get the job right up to the eve of the PDP National Convention.

But powerful forces were out to undermine Odili. On the night of December 16, 2006 – the day before the PDP was to pick its presidential and vice presidential candidates for the election of 2007 – six men gathered at the Abuja home of Senator Andy Uba, then a Senior Special Assistant on

Domestic Affairs to Obasanjo. Apart from Uba himself, the group consisted of Aliko Dangote – Nigeria's richest man – the EFCC Chairman, Nuhu Ribadu, former Delta State governor, Chief James Ibori, his Kwara State counterpart Dr Bukola Saraki, and Zenon Oil Chairman Femi Otedola. They were there to discuss only one thing: how to stop Peter Odili being announced as Yar'Adua's running mate the very next day.

They were aware that time was short. Odili's name had already been written into the acceptance speech to be read by Yar'Adua at the convention location, Abuja's Eagle Square. The only way to derail his appointment would be to publicise the allegations about corruption in as high profile a manner as possible. To do this, they concluded, they would need the services of Olusegun Adeniyi, then the editor of the country's leading newspaper, ThisDay. It was Dangote who made the call and Adeniyi, who was not about to turn down an invitation from such an influential personage, readily agreed to join them.

Recalling what happened next a few years later, Adeniyi wrote: "Since my arrival did not change the tone of discussion, it was easy for me to keep abreast of what the issue was: then Rivers State governor, Dr. Peter Odili, had been selected by President Olusegun Obasanjo as running mate to his anointed PDP presidential candidate, Alhaji Umaru Musa Yar'Adua… The essence of the gathering was to stop Odili from becoming Yar'Adua's running mate on grounds of alleged corruption."

By this time Odili had a reputation as one of the more controversial Governors in Nigerian history, and when it had been revealed that he had budgeted more for his office expenses than education in his state a media storm ensued. The EFCC investigated Odili over misuse of public funds to the tune of N100 billion. The investigation heralded no charges, but was sufficient to stall the Governor's political ambitions.

Adeniyi's account continued: "When I asked why I was invited to the meeting, they said they had an exclusive story for ThisDay which would highlight allegations of corruption against Odili but with a caveat: it had to be published in next morning's edition of the newspaper. The evidence was to be supplied by Ribadu who held a file containing the documents. While I considered the proposition somewhat ridiculous, I also wondered how a ThisDay publication could affect the decision to make Odili the running mate. It was then they explained what was going on".[3]

The conspirators' plan worked perfectly. The story ws published and Ribadu convinced Obasanjo of the former Governor's unsuitability as a vice presidential candidate and he was quickly taken off the ticket. In an interview later with Elendureports.com entitled "Odili is a Crook", Ribadu said: "Peter Odili is smart, a gangster. He is a crook we know but we cannot trace anything to him. There are a couple of them like that". Adeniyi, meanwhile, was rewarded with the post of Special Adviser on Communications to Yar'Adua on 30 May, 2007, a position he held until the president died. He is currently chairman of ThisDay's editorial board.

In his own biography, "Conscience and History: My Story", Odili denied the allegations and revealed that he was only too aware of how close he had come to being Vice President. He had even seen an advance copy of Yar'Adua's acceptance speech naming him as the president's running mate. He was dramatically dropped at the Convention venue in Abuja, he explained, through "a complex power game" between Obasanjo and Ribadu.

With Odili out of the picture the PDP was quickly running out of options. But Obasanjo did not budge – Yar'Adua's vice president needed to be someone from the Delta. Jonathan's credentials were pretty much impeccable. He came from the heart of the oil-producing region, was untainted by corruption, had proven his party loyalty in the Alamieyeseigha saga, and he appeared to be someone that they could control.

But, according to Edwin Clark, the former Minister of Information and fellow Niger Delta indigene, Jonathan's first reaction when he was asked to be Yar'Adua's running mate was to turn it down. Once again, after being sweet-talked by tribal elders, in the end he accepted. The Yar'Adua/Jonathan ticket duly won, and on May 29, 2007, he was inaugurated as Nigeria's Vice President.

Goodluck Jonathan has travelled an extraordinary journey from a very anonymous deputy in a provincial state, to President. He became Governor without necessarily pushing for it, or wanting it. Then he became Vice President without desiring or lobbying for it. Jonathan was a blank canvas, exactly what most Presidents want from their deputy. As one columnist put it, "He was the kind of person who rose without a trace."

Not everyone agrees that Jonathan's appointment can be attributed entirely to an accident of fate, however. While events may have worked in his favour, it is partly down to Jonathan's judgement that he was in the right place at the right time. This is certainly the view of Ken Saro-Wiwa Jr and he is very definitely a man worth listening to. As the son of a prominent human rights activist whose execution at the hands of the Abacha regime caused a global furore, he was brought up steeped in Nigerian politics and now serves as Senior Special Assistant to the President on International Media and Civil Society.

"What has always struck me as one of Jonathan's best attributes is timing," he says. "People always tend to underestimate him, but he always keeps his head cool. I have served three Presidents. With Obasanjo, he intimidated you with his presence and he dominated the space. Yar'Adua intimidated you with his silence and then sucked the air out of the room. Now Jonathan is quite shy, but when the real Jonathan comes out you are quite taken aback. He has a native intelligence, and he can see through the situation. He is often criticised for things he has not done, or not acted, but he is looking three steps ahead. That's what I mean by native intelligence, and in Nigerian politics it is necessary in order to survive. But his calm manner confuses Nigerians who are used to big men who shout. The worst thing you can do is to underestimate Jonathan. He has an incredible gift of timing."

Like his stint as a Deputy Governor, Jonathan's time as Vice President was largely spent outside of the limelight. He was given free rein to manage the situation in the Delta, but was otherwise kept away from any real decision-making. It is telling that when the US Embassy in Nigeria cabled a list to Washington of the country's most influential people in October 2008, Jonathan's name was not on the list. Instead there were people such as David Mark, the President of the Senate of Nigeria and Senator for the Benue State constituency, as well as a number of (then) state governors, including Ahmed Shekarau and Bukola Saraki.

Olusegun Adeniyi, the former spokesperson of late President Yar'Adua, narrates another interesting story: "As early in the administration as December 2007, a group of women had paid [Patience Jonathan] a visit, and in the course of the discussion, one had asked: "How is Oga? [Jonathan]" To this Mrs. Jonathan replied, "My husband is in the office reading newspapers." Then she added rather sarcastically: "Abi no be newspaper Turai [Mrs. Yar'Adua] say make im dey read?" – pidgin that approximates as insinuating even then perhaps it was Yar'Adua's wife, Turai, who was really calling the shots, telling the President's deputy how he should be spending his time."" [4]

One of the most fascinating insider accounts of life in State House during Yar'Adua's administration is offered by Adeniyi, the man who helped to bring down Odili. In his book Power, Politics and Death, Adeniyi portrays his former boss in a largely flattering light, but he also offers an insight into the precarious nature of democracy in Nigeria at the time. "If we will be honest with ourselves, we all know how we rig elections in this country," Adeniyi quotes Yar'Adua as saying during a closed-door meeting in January 2008. "We compromise the security agencies, we pay the electoral officials and party agents while on the eve of the election we merely distribute logistics all designed to buy the vote."

As the president's health began to fail, he began to lose his grip on power. Soldiers would be deployed without proper authorization, for example. In the absence of strong leadership, power struggles grew in intensity and rumours of a possible coup floated among the elite. In Yar'Adua's final months in office, one figure in particular came to the fore. The president's wife, Turai, acquired the image of a Lady Macbeth hungry for power and determined to loot the country's coffers while she still had the chance. She practically held the Government in a lockdown through her insistence on keeping her husband in office even when Yar'Adua had reportedly lost the capacity to communicate or make any rational decisions. According to the Nigerian newspaper Next, quoting unnamed sources from the hospital in Jeddah, towards the end Yar'Adua was "seriously brain-damaged and unable to recognise anyone including his wife".

By February 9, 2010, the president's condition was so bad that Jonathan assumed office as Nigeria's Acting President by virtue of a National Assembly resolution. Three months later, Yar'Adua died and the very next day – May 6 2010 – Jonathan was sworn in as the President and Commander-in-chief of the Armed Forces.

In a country where would-be politicians spend millions of dollars campaigning, Jonathan had never actively sought or hustled for political office. He had simply positioned himself well and patiently waited for events to unfold in his favour. Despite his meteoric rise from being a State Deputy Governor, State Governor, Vice President and then President, the presidential election of 2011 was Jonathan's very first contest for elected office since becoming a politician in 1998.

As a result, he was not well known to the public at large. This is a deficit he could have addressed by ramping up his media appearances but that is not his way, according to Ken Saro-Wiwa Jr. "As a President he is too honest," he explains. "Jonathan answers the question he is asked. He is not like other politicians. Then I cannot say that media appearances are his strongest point. Media in Nigeria is fierce, they go in for the kill. The Jonathan that I know, who can sit down and do an insightful interview with Christine Amanpour on CNN or calmly hold the stage at the World Economic Forum, rarely gets a chance to do that at home in Nigeria. He himself doesn't shy away from the media though. If he hears about an interview he almost always says yes. It is often the people around him who prevent it. The apparatus around the President, in a way, stops you from actually seeing the President. People who do get to see him are always surprised. In person he is so different the way he is portrayed by the media. It is a lot of mediated rubbish, but then again that is the nature of the game."

Presidents generally take power with a First Lady in tow and Jonathan was no exception. Some, like Mrs Obasanjo did, keep a low profile, while others, such as Mrs Yar'Adua, are perceived to be among the President's closest advisors. Patience Jonathan appears to fit into neither camp.

"In many ways his wife is more a politician than he is,"

says Saro-Wiwa Jr. "She is often criticised but I think she is an asset to him. She connects with people. Oronto Douglas [Special Adviser to the President] always says that 'She can give you the eba and soup explanation' that everyone understands."

For the uninitiated eba – or garri – is made from grated cassava, mixed with water to form a doughy substance and rolled into balls to eat with soup. It is one of the most popular dishes in Nigeria. So, "the eba and soup explanation" is one that is comprehensible to the most unsophisticated listener.

Saro-Wiwa Jr adds: " She is a strong woman, but in terms of the couple it works. They have been through just about every challenge that Nigerian politics can throw at them."

Chapter Two

MAKING OF A PRESIDENT

It is a truism that Goodluck Jonathan became President of Nigeria due to circumstance rather than vaulted ambition. But the route to high office was a difficult one that involved navigating his way through the minefield of Nigerian politics and over the objections of many who never wanted him to get the job.

Goodluck Jonathan's accession to power was due to the sudden death of his predecessor, Umaru Yar'Adua, who died in 2010 while in office. However, it was not a clean transition. In order to take up his rightful constitutional position, Jonathan had to overcome the political plotting and scheming of Yar'Adua's aides who were loath to surrender the biggest prize in African politics – the Presidency of Nigeria.

Further buttressing this was the belief by many politicians in the north of Nigeria that, as a Southerner, Jonathan had no right to the Presidency. Under an informal power sharing arrangement within the ruling People's Democratic Party, the Presidency belonged to the North. Olusegun Obasanjo, a Yoruba from the Southwest, had been President from 1999 to 2007, the first eight years after the end of military rule. After Obasanjo it was the North's turn, but this was turned on its head when Yar 'Adua got so sick only two and a half years into his Presidency that he could no longer discharge his duties.

As Vice President, Jonathan was constitutionally next in line for the Presidency, and was to lead the country in Yar 'Adua's absence, but even before the death of the President, a number of political groups combined to try stop the then Deputy President from even becoming the Acting President.

Those who most actively sought to thwart Jonathan's influence during Yar'Adua's long illness included the former President's aide-de-camp, Colonel Mustapha Onudieva, and his Chief Security Officer, Yusuf Tilde.

In late November 2009, President Yar'Adua, aged just 58, was flown to Saudi Arabia for special treatment amidst his deteriorating health. His political career had been dominated by uncertainty over his health. For much of his life he suffered from asthma and eczema and in 2002, while Governor of Katsina, spent several months abroad to have a kidney transplant.

Despite his recurrent health problems and without a strong political base in the north of Nigeria, Yar'Adua was selected by President Obasanjo as his anointed successor at a party convention in 2006 with the then unknown Jonathan as the surprise choice as his running mate. But ill health and medical trips to Saudi Arabia and Switzerland dominated his Presidency and in late 2009 he returned to Jeddah to be treated for pericarditis – an inflammation of the membrane protecting the heart.

Back home Yar 'Adua's extended absence made many

Nigerians nervous and anxious about the state of the nation. As their President lay in a private clinic in Jeddah, slowly dying, apparently having suffered a stroke and unable to communicate or even perform the most basic tasks, there were repeated calls for executive powers to be formally transferred to Jonathan, his deputy. A constitutional crisis was looming.

The problem was that there was no provision in the constitution to deal with a situation when the president was too ill to sign off priorities like the annual budget. There was a feeling that no one was in charge, and that the Vice President did not have the authority to run the country. Jonathan's political enemies saw this as an opportunity to hijack the process, exploit the uncertainty and set up an interim government in order to prevent him from taking over

As Vice President, Jonathan assumed powers to administer the basic running of the country. But there was no official communication from the National Assembly, or from Yar'Adua himself. And so officially Nigeria did not have a President. "As Vice President I could handle certain roles of the Presidency, but I could not assume the role of Commander In Chief", recalled Jonathan. "There is only one Commander In Chief and that's the President. There was no such thing as 'Acting Commander In Chief'. I could assume the legislative and the executive responsibilities, but the reality was such that there was no Commander In Chief during Yar'Adua's absence. And so the President was incapacitated. There was no one to command the troops, and no one with the right authority who could demand them to go and fight if required"

Meanwhile, Nigeria was consumed by an atmosphere of tension, rumours of a military coup, and there were even death threats to the President. "Three friends of mine arranged different places for me to sleep at night", recalled Jonathan. "They did not even want me to sleep in the State House. They were so afraid for my safety, and that the military would take over. But I said that in that case I would prefer to die in the state house, rather than hide somewhere else. Also, if I left and something happened, there would be so many stories and conspiracy theories and no one would know why I left. If they were going to assassinate me, it would be better if I sleep in the state house and then it will all be clear for everyone to see. But if I slept somewhere else, I know that nothing would be clear. The question of death, it is real but it comes with this job. You cannot run away from it. If it comes, I will be ready for it."

In his absence Yar'Adua's closest confidantes – his wife Turai, Onudieva and Tilde – hijacked the running of the country. Government became slow and bureaucratic – even by Nigerian standards – and Yar'Adua was dubbed "Baba Go Slow" (Baba had been the nickname of his predecessor, Olusegun Obasanjo, for his "fatherly" style of governing).

This was later confirmed by President Yar'Adua's own spokesperson, Olusegun Adeniyi, who chronicled the power struggles within the government during his final months in office. In his book "Power, Politics and Death", Adeniyi states that as far as Turai, Onudieva and Tilde were concerned, the President could remain in his sick bed in Saudi Arabia for as long Nigerians could tolerate it, so they could consolidate their grip on power: "For at least six months before he finally passed on, President Yar'Adua was no longer in charge of himself to say nothing of the country. This made the three people who surrounded him – Turai, Onudieva and Tilde – the actual leaders of the country".

As concerns mounted and Yar'Adua remained silent on transferring power to his Vice President, members of the National Assembly took matters into their own hands. On January 13, 2010, a federal court handed Jonathan the power to administer state affairs and assume the role of Commander in Chief while President Yar'Adua received medical treatment in Saudi Arabia. The following month, an extraordinary National Assembly vote confirmed these powers, which they described as essential to "peace, order and good government."

After Jonathan was given the mandate to govern, a semblance of security and stability returned. "There really was only one option if Nigeria was to consolidate its emergence out of military rule", according to one insider close to the events. "To uphold the constitution there could really only be one outcome. Jonathan took a lot of the heat out of the debate. He worked patiently with the national assembly to come up with a 'doctrine of necessity', basically saying there might not be a law, but this is what should happen. So Jonathan was given the Executive Authority before Yar'Adua's death by the National Assembly, and he actually pushed through some changes. For example, he sacked Yar'Adua's Attorney General, one of the most notorious of the advisors of the previous regime."

But incredibly, Jonathan – who was President in all but

name – was never informed when Yar 'Adua secretly returned to Nigeria in the dark early hours of 24 February 2010. While two planes from Jeddah landed at Nnamdi Azikiwe International Airport in Abuja, an ambulance was waiting on the tarmac and quickly dispatched the ailing Yar'Adua to hospital his vice-president had no idea.

Instead Jonathan woke later that morning to find a city surrounded by the military. That could only mean one thing, he thought: Yar'Adua was back. He had not been consulted about the army's deployment. Instead he found out, like the rest of the Abuja citizens, when he saw the streets around Yar'Adua's villa surrounded by armoured vehicles. "Again it was a very unusual situation", reflected Jonathan. "Now you had an acting President and a President in the same country. People were confused. Again there was uncertainty of who was in charge. It was a very anomalous situation that created confusion. It is dangerous to rush these things so I remained calm and I waited."

In the streets of Lagos and Abuja, there was acute anxiety and uncertainty. Nobody knew what was happening or who was in charge. Jonathan's advisors suspected a coup. "I was a little concerned that the military would see the opportunity to strike", recalled Oronto Douglas, a Special Adviser to Jonathan on Strategy. "But after eight years of unbroken democracy it would be difficult. Jonathan remained calm and waited. It was a real testament to his judgement, and I remember at the time Tony Blair expressed his awe in how Jonathan handled the situation. If he seized power, which he was entitled to, it would have sent a bad message to the North. But he didn't. Instead he waited and he succeeded."

Later that evening Jonathan visited Yar'Adua at the presidential villa, but he was immediately denied access. He was greeted by the President's wife, Hajiya Turai, who stopped him at the door, saying Yar'Adua was too weak to receive any visitors. A startled Jonathan was then told that his words and wishes would be conveyed by the Yar'Adua's aides.

At that point Yar'Adua had not been seen in public for three months – since November 23, 2009, the day before he was flown abroad for his medical treatment. His Aide-de-Camp Colonel Onudieva and his Chief Security Officer, Yusuf Tilde, now played a key role in keeping Yar'Adua away from public officials since his return, and any inquiries into the President's health were unceremoniously turned away. There was now a power struggle between Onudieva and Tilde and Jonathan.

This was illustrated only hours after Yar'Adua's return when Onudieva positioned himself behind the President's seat in anticipation of his boss chairing that day's Federal Executive Council meeting. This chair had been occupied by Jonathan since 13 January 2010, as acting President and aides looked on nervously – and with a hint of dark amusement – to see what would happen if Jonathan attempted to occupy the chair. A potential clash was averted when neither Yar'Adua nor Jonathan turned up for the meeting, which was cancelled. But it was not clear if Onudieva would have prevented Jonathan from taking the president's seat if he attempted to sit down.

By March 2010, President Yar'Adua could barely function. He could no longer walk out of his bedroom and staged photo opportunities with visiting religious leaders, which only drew attention to his declining health. He was often propped up like a stuffed teddy bear each time he made a public appearance. In effect, he was quarantined and hidden away like a damaged museum piece. He would be wheeled out publicly when required to do so, but in reality could not perform the simplest of state functions.

One report even claimed that the President was secretly brain dead. According to Dele Olojede, editor of the Nigerian newspaper NEXT: [1][2]

"President Umaru Yar'Adua is seriously brain damaged, is not able to recognise anyone, including his wife Turai, and can no longer perform the functions of the office of the president, according to multiple sources who have spoken to NEXT on Sunday. But this fact, which has left a nation of 150 million people rudderless and its government in disarray, is being concealed from the public directly and energetically by the First Lady.

"Turai Yar'Adua has barred all but two security and one civilian aides, and a legislator from having access to the president in a two-tier power loop of which she is the organising principal"

This state of affairs was crystallised when Jonathan tried to sack Onudieva and Tilde and was fiercely resisted by the ailing president's wife on the grounds that she had "no idea how to explain it" to her husband. She also raised concerns over what people might say "should anything happen" to the President in the event of the dismissal of his trusted aides.

By 14 April 2010, Jonathan had still not seen Yar 'Adua, and only communicated with the President via his wife, and his aides, Onudieva and Tilde. "The thinking of the family is that they should isolate him from most of the key actors in government", he told CNN. "I have not seen him. The Senate president has not seen him, and at every single government function". When asked whether that caused anxiety amongst the people, he replied: "Yes, it does. Obviously, it does, but we cannot influence his family's thinking". He added that he was frustrated that he was barred from seeing the President but decided not to force the issue.

On the night that President Yar' Adua died – 5 May 2010 – his wife sent a message to Jonathan: "Your brother is dead, come and see him". In the middle of the night, accompanied by the Speaker of the House of Representatives, Jonathan arrived at the villa and was greeted by Yar' Adua's wife. "You should go up and see him", she said. But the Speaker replied nervously: "No, I cannot see a dead body". Jonathan felt compelled to go upstairs but then hesitated and a remarkable thought crossed his mind: "Is this a set up or a trap, for them to also take my life?"

Jonathan overcame his last-minute anxiety, walked upstairs and saw the President lying down in the bed in the master bedroom. On seeing his dead body, he was overcome by sadness and broke down and wept. He acknowledged that Yar'Adua did not just die. He had endured prolonged physical pain, and the events leading up to his death had been orchestrated and manipulated. In the end Yar'Adua had been but a pawn in a cruel power game. "Yes, I was very upset", he said. "We humans are mere mortals and will die, yes, but the circumstances of his death were sad. My brother had died."

Politically, Jonathan's immediate reaction to the death was that it could result in chaos and insurrection. "While Yar 'Adua was sick some thought that he was going to recover", he recalled. "But now he was dead, I was worried it would push the country into crisis, and the army would take over. And if Nigeria would derail again into military dictatorship the sub-region would be gone. There would be crisis in the entire region. I was thinking is Africa drifting now? If military dictatorship succeeds in Nigeria, the continent is gone too, and Nigeria would drag the continent down. My priority was to stabilise the government and whether I could cope with uniting the country.

"I was not worried about running the country. I knew I could do that. I had already been running the country for a very long time. No, the issue was more 'how would people react.' The issue was not whether I had been doing well. No, the issue was 'it was our own turn in the north' and 'this person must not be there'. So how do you manage that complex situation? That was drifting through my head that night. The stability of the country was now paramount"

The next morning, 6 May 2010, Jonathan was sworn in as President in a brief inaugural ceremony, presided over by the Secretary General, Yayale Ahmed, and the Chief Justice, Aloysius Katsina-Alu. A Muslim cleric and a Reverend Father delivered the opening prayers during a solemn occasion.

The ceremony was not open to the public but it was

televised. Jonathan wore his customary wide-brimmed hat, and a sash bearing the national colours of green and white. In his traditional Bayelsa attire, he has sometimes been criticised for looking out of place, in contrast to other world leaders in their sober grey suits. But his attire was no surprise in Nigeria, where it has long been customary for political leaders to wear traditional clothes on formal occasions – the flowing 'agbadas' of Yoruba leaders from the south-west or the 'babban riga' of the politicians from the North. But less familiar was Jonathan's tunic and hat, a reflection of his roots in a small minority population within a marginalised part of the country. But as he rose to speak in the Aso Rock presidential villa in Abuja, national conciliation was on his mind:

"President Yar'Adua's contribution to political development and good governance would never be forgotten. He will therefore always occupy a pride of place in the political history of our dear Nation. He was a man of great personal integrity, deep devotion to God and outstanding humility. In all his public service, he displayed uncommon commitment to the peace, progress and unity of our country. He has left for us a profound legacy that provides a firm foundation for Nigeria's future. His exit has therefore created a huge vacuum in his personal contributions to the political growth and development of our nation. I have lost not just a boss but a good friend and brother.

"Having taken the oath of office in line with the Nigerian Constitution, under these very sad and unusual circumstances, I urge all fellow citizens to remain steadfast and committed to the values and aspirations of our nation. While this is a major burden on me and indeed the entire nation, we must in the midst of such great adversity continue to garner our collective efforts towards upholding the values, which our departed leader represented.

"In this regard our total commitment to Good Governance, Electoral Reform and the fight against Corruption would be pursued with greater vigour. As I had stated time and again, we must enshrine the best standards in our democratic practice. One of the true tests would be to ensure that all votes count and are counted in the upcoming General Elections. Similarly the effort at ensuring the sustenance of peace and development in the Niger Delta as well as the security of life and property around the entire country would be of top most priority in the remaining period of this administration"

Watching closely and listening carefully during his speech were powerful and influential figures within the Yar'Adua administration, such as Bukola Saraki [former Governor of Kwara State], James Ibori [later jailed for 13 years for money laundering], Tanimu Yakubu [Yar'Adua's former Chief Economic Adviser], General Dambazu [Chief of Army Staff], and Michael Aondoakaa [the Justice Minister and Attorney General]. They had all, in one way or another, been involved in a government cover-up designed to hide the severity of the former President's condition.

These former governors, particularly Ibori and Saraki, had wielded enormous power during the Yar'Adua administration, notably the controversial removal of Mallam

Nuhu Ribadu, the pioneering chairman of the Economic and Financial Crimes Commission (EFCC). Ribadu was replaced by Farida Waziri, later herself investigated by the Independent Corrupt Practices Commission (ICPC). This was heavily criticised by former President Obasanjo who said the appointment of Waziri slowed down the fight against corruption in the country:

"I know that the woman they brought in to replace Ribadu (Farida Waziri) was not the right person for that job, because I understood that one of those who head-hunted her was James Ibori. If James Ibori, who is now in a U.K. prison for fraud, head-hunted somebody who will fight corruption in Nigeria, then you can understand my concern".[3] [4]

Jonathan's unexpected rise was opposed by factions within the ruling People's Democratic Party (PDP) who ensured that he was kept well outside the inner circles of power during his time as Vice President. The only policy area where he had been given free reign was the crisis in the oil-rich Niger Delta where he travelled there regularly, by himself, and without any security. "He trusted that his own people wouldn't hurt him", said one aide.

As Vice President, Jonathan engaged in efforts to negotiate with the militants in the Delta, who were fighting against the oil companies operating in the region. He proposed an amnesty programme for the insurgents, whereby if they surrendered their weapons they would be offered training to integrate back into society. This was an economic as well as a security prerogative. Prior to this initiative the production in the Delta had fallen dramatically to 800,000 barrels per day, from an original capacity of more than 2 million.

In many ways Jonathan's good luck and ascent to the Presidency is a product of his origins in the south. When Yar'Adua died, the party leadership wanted a replacement from the north, and there is a theory that Jonathan was only "given" the Presidency in order to prevent a breakdown in the Delta negotiations. The PDP believed that without Jonathan the situation in the Delta would have deteriorated and stripped the country and its elite from much needed and desired revenue. Jonathan fitted the bill and appeared harmless with his non-confrontational and professorial approach.

Like President Putin's rise to power in Russia, the power brokers were eventually persuaded that they could "handle" Jonathan for a year or so, while they found a suitable replacement from the north. In constitutional terms, it would have been extremely awkward to find any pretext for passing over the Vice-President to succeed Yar'Adua, given that his primary role was to stand in if the President dies or is indisposed.

Jonathan's unassuming manner resulted in him being under-estimated, "I first met Jonathan in 2005", said one well-connected international consultant. "He was very softly spoken and is not one of those Nigerians who went to private school in England and travels the world. I think he has a lot more in common with ordinary Nigerians than a lot of his peers. I think his ambitions were quite modest."

Jonathan had been proposed as candidate for Vice

President so that the PDP would be seen as addressing the neglected oil-producing region of Nigeria. The more established political leaders in the region had a polarising influence, carried a great deal of baggage and so helped cancel one another out. By including Jonathan in the administration, they hoped to placate the rising chaos in the Delta. For them Jonathan merely served a short-term political purpose.

In office Jonathan has been portrayed as detached and weak. A former US Ambassador to Nigeria once described him as having an "underwhelming personality", according to diplomatic cables obtained by WikiLeaks. But sources close to Jonathan convey a very different impression. They describe him as "patient, intelligent and deliberate". One close aide said:

"In the jungle there are many animals. Jonathan is the Eagle. He calmly sits and waits for the right time to strike. You can wave and shout at him, but he will still wait. He is a man that only takes deliberate action. Some times this frustrates his associates and opponents alike. There are many lions and hippos in Nigeria's political establishment. They all got overexcited at the prospect of becoming President. They push hard and they exhaust and expose themselves in the process. But Jonathan just waited. He understood how the system worked and let it have its course. He remained calm. The Nigerian constitution would grant him the Presidency upon Yar'Adua's death. There was no need for politics"

When asked by CNN about the Machiavellian power plays in the PDP, Jonathan was confident that the system would override the bickering in the party. "Do you believe that those around him are trying to undermine you or your new cabinet?" he was asked. "I wouldn't say they are trying to undermine me, but the laws of the land are very clear", he replied. " And, of course, that is why in the first place the constitution is designed for two people to be in charge of government at every time, one superior and one inferior"

Much of Jonathan's actions – which have been criticised as inactions by his opponents – can be attributed to a belief in the inherent functioning of Nigeria's political system separate from the whim of the Presidency. And so instead of prosecuting selected high profile figures for fraud and theft – which was the modus operandi of the Obasanjo administration and so creating perceptions of vendettas – Jonathan talks about eliminating the "centres of corruption". By privatising the state institutions that breed corruption, Jonathan believed that this would exterminate the source of the disease.

But this strategy has been criticised by opponents as a naïve, idealistic – if touching – confidence in a system that is already so corroded and beyond repair. But the President has shown no signs of self-doubt. He maintains that results can only be delivered by a shift in culture, promoted by the strengthening of institutions, the elimination of opportunity and the application of due process of law. In a nation accustomed to the quick fix, he believes the problem can only be solved by a long-term approach.

The new President's main challenge was to resolve the dispute in the Delta region, from where oil and gas exports generate more than 90 per cent of foreign exchange earnings. This was Jonathan's trump card – he was from the Niger Delta and understood their frustrations and demands for recognition while deploring their brutal methods. It was a historic advantage and based on his roots. "He reached this position largely due to where he is from", noted one aide. "And so why should he conform and ignore his heritage? Jonathan is a proud Nigerian from the Delta who wants to make a difference"

Before his rise to power Jonathan never mingled with the rich and mighty, in fact before he became President Jonathan had never left Nigeria. "It is interesting to look at Jonathan's travels before and after 2010", said one source close to the Presidency. "He has probably done more in the last five years than he has in the 50 years before that. How do you adapt to this world where you have no real privacy or time. Some people rise with it, like Obasanjo, I don't know with Jonathan. I think his ambitions were very modest."

The unlikely political ascent of this obscure son of a rural canoe-carver and fisherman from the oil-producing south, due to a series of coincidences and mishaps, occurred almost in spite of him, according to aides and analysts. "He's not obsessed with power," said Samuel Amadi, "He doesn't have the usual swagger of Nigerian politicians."

Jonathan's track record and diffident benign manner immediately raised questions whether he possessed the requisite toughness to negotiate the minefield that is political life in Nigeria. He was confronted by formidable challenges – 36 powerful state governors, some very corrupt who controlled immense oil-fuelled budgets, a large unruly military establishment that has spent much of Nigeria's 50 years of independence meddling in politics and warring factions of northern politicians resentful that one of their own, Yar'Adua, had been prematurely removed before the 2011 elections in favour of a southerner.

Jonathan's humility and quiet policy of conciliation contrasts starkly with the prevailing atmosphere of Nigeria – brash, loud, chaotic, bombastic and dynamic. Until his Presidency, Nigerian politics has been intricately woven around political and military authoritarianism reinforced by brute force.

But by the 2011 election the prevailing mood and atmosphere was different – less shrill, more thoughtful. It was also notable for an improvement in the way the ballot was conducted. Elections in Nigeria had been notorious for being manipulated and fraudulent. When Jonathan became President the previous year his priorities were to stabilize the country but also clean up its political institutions. "There was a fear of coup and mutiny", he recalled. "And so my first commitment was how to stabilise the country. My next focus was how to conduct an election that is free and fair, because if I had manufactured an election in my favour there would have been a coup and they could have justified it. That is why we have a major war against corruption, to enable free, fair and transparent elections in Nigeria"

Nigeria became independent in 1960, leaving an uneasy federation of three powerful regional governments under the stewardship of a central administration. There were tensions between the Hausa-Fulani in the North, the Yoruba in the West and the Igbo in the East. And within these regions there was tension and disputes over representation and access to resources between majority and minority groups.

In January 1966, as corruption escalated and competition for power became more fierce, young army officers attempted a bloody coup. Many politicians were killed, notably Tafawa Balewa, the Prime Minister, and Ahmadu Bello, Premier of the Northern Region. The coup collapsed but civilian rule was not restored and the seeds of the slide towards civil war were sewn. General Johnson Aguiyi-Ironsi, the military commander, tried to deal with the tensions that led to the attempted coup by abolishing regional governments in favour of a unitary state. But others regarded this as a grab for power – like several of the coup plotters, Ironsi was an Igbo from the East. Within six months there was a bloody mutiny and counter coup led by Northern army officers.

The fall-out of this coup in July 1966 was pogroms and ethnic cleansing in cities across the country. The new dictator, General Gowon, failed to reach an agreement with Brigadier Ojukwu in the East and so the stage was set for a civil war that would last nearly three years and cost nearly a million lives – the infamous Biafran war. Faced with the demands for secession by the Biafrans, the mantra of the federal government was to keep Nigeria united as one nation – a catchy jingle on federal radio endlessly repeated "to keep Nigeria one is a task that must be done." In a bid to win over hearts and minds, Gowon proposed the abolition of regional governments and the establishment of a 12-state federation to accommodate the aspirations of minority groups in the Niger Delta and Middle Belt of central Nigeria.

Gowon was in turn overthrown in 1975 by officers impatient at the slow pace of reform to restore civilian government – and perhaps privately a little impatient to secure a slice of Nigeria's then booming oil economy. But efforts to create a sustainable democracy remained elusive for a further generation, marked by more coups – successful and failed – a brief ill-fated experiment with civilian rule and years of dictatorship and international isolation until 1999.

The transition from military rule has not been easy. There remain serious problems with political governance, accountability and representation. But the Fourth Republic has proved more enduring. Goodluck Jonathan is Nigeria's third consecutively elected President – an unprecedented sequence of elections. And even before his victory in the 2011 election, Nigeria had achieved something which most commentators would not have thought possible – when Yar'Adua's incapacity resulted in a unique constitutional crisis, the new President was sworn in without a coup or disruption or chaos.

Jonathan did not seize power in a coup, unlike many of his predecessors. He was not an army man, but a mild-mannered academic in a black fedora from the Niger Delta who happened to be in the right place at the right time. He had been a heartbeat away from the Presidency and when destiny called, he stood up to the mark.

Chapter Three

MYTHS AND REALITIES

In the early 1990s an American relationship counsellor published a bestseller called 'Men Are from Mars, Women Are From Venus'. The thesis was that men and women live on very different planets. Phillip van Niekerk, former editor of the Mail & Guardian in South Africa and now an analyst on West Africa, reckons that observers of contemporary Nigeria fall into similarly distinct camps. Speaking at an event hosted by the Atlantic Council in 2012, he said: "How people view Nigeria is so vastly at a dissonance that you could say one lot is living on Pluto and the other one on Mercury. Pluto is a very cold, dark place, and viewed from there, Nigeria is an unmitigated disaster and a hell of corruption, rigged elections and an incompetent, sectarian, and predatory government. Residents of Pluto are always convinced that Nigeria is just about to go over a cliff." According to van Niekerk, the vocabulary of the "Plutocrats" is limited to terms such as "state failures" and "civil war."

Viewed from a quite different position in the solar system, however, the outlook for Nigeria is much brighter. Van Niekerk continued: "From the sunnier Mercury, Nigeria is the waking giant of Africa. We've seen a decade of unparalleled growth. Revolutions in retail, mobile phones, in banking, and this has unlocked the dynamism of Nigerian people, and given rise to a great economic power that is only years away from surpassing my own country, South Africa, as the largest economy on the continent."

So what explains these contradictory viewpoints that are so far at variance? As the Plutocrats outnumber the Mercunauts, at least in the West, it makes sense to analyse their position first.

A conventional, well-rehearsed narrative portrays Nigeria as a very bleak place on a very dark continent. It is usually described as a country that suffers from dysfunctional government and an absence of the rule of law. Scholars say that poverty is getting worse and the poverty gap between the poor South and the much poorer North, is getting bigger. Critics complain of an adversarial security apparatus, where the army and police often struggle to present themselves as the honest guardians of a long suffering silent majority. Some have gone so far as to suggest that, at least at some level, Boko Haram is the most visible element of an indigenous uprising spawned by the poverty and official corruption that pervades parts of the North. At the same time, according to the same narrative, disaffected elements in the Niger Delta, in the South, are re-grouping because the grievances in the region have never been properly addressed. In sum, Nigeria is polarised along religious and ethnic lines and more and more of its citizens across the country feel alienated from a state that they regard as corrupt.

In his book, "Nigeria: Dancing on the Brink", John

Campbell, US ambassador to Nigeria between 2004 and 2007, predicted that Nigeria would collapse and disintegrate into several countries along ethnic and cultural lines by 2015. "Popular alienation and a fragmented establishment have contributed to Nigeria becoming one of the most religious and, at the same time, one of the most violent countries in the world," he writes.

According to Campbell, it is now only a question of time until doomsday and "one of the reasons why Nigeria has danced on the brink and not fallen over it [yet] is there has been a kind of unity amongst the elites all over the country. Part of that is self-interest. It is, after all, a united Nigeria that gives them access to the immense amounts of oil revenue."

Peter Lewis, Director of African Studies at the Paul H. Nitze School of Advanced Studies of Johns Hopkins University, paints a similar picture. In his paper, "The Dysfunctional State of Nigeria", he portrays what he perceives as the continuous decline in the country:

"There is no question... that Nigeria has failed profoundly as a state, a nation, and an economy. Central authorities cannot provide stable governance, in the sense of effective legitimate rule and essential public goods. The country's boundaries may provisionally be settled, but the basis of political community—the idea of Nigeria—is fiercely contested. Economically, Nigeria has experienced a steady decline since the oil windfall peaked more than twenty years ago. Slow growth and a rapidly rising population have yielded dramatic increases in poverty.

"The country's continued economic stagnation and

endemic corruption impede US commercial relations with Nigeria and more generally hinder economic development in West Africa. Weak governance and economic frailty also underlie the leading irritants in the US- Nigerian relationship: narcotics trafficking, financial fraud, and money laundering. In addition, the rising incidence of HIV-AIDS in Nigeria accentuates humanitarian problems and the health risks inherent in global interactions."

This is the narrative that is most commonly associated with Nigeria.

But the foundations are somewhat flimsy. As Ambassador Campbell himself concedes: "Except for the experts, most of us do not know much about Nigeria, and what we do know is based on Lagos, and to a lesser extent Abuja, and neither of those cities are representative of the country." His own predictions of Nigeria's imminent demise appear set to be proved premature.

In 2011, ahead of the presidential elections that would pit Jonathan against Northern kingpin Muhammadu Buhari, Campbell contributed an article to the Huffington Post. Under the headline, "Why Nigeria's North-South Distinction Is Important", he wrote: "In general, control of the state has been accomplished through various forms of power sharing. Within the ruling People's Democratic Party, from 1999 to 2011, Nigerian elites reached an informal agreement, often referred to as 'zoning'. It provided for the rotation of the presidency between the North and the South. When the president was a southern Christian, the vice president was a northern Muslim, and vice versa.

"It was the South's turn with Olusegun Obasanjo from 1999 to 2007, and it was supposed to be the North's until 2015. However, following northern president Yar'Adua's death in office, his southern vice president, Goodluck Jonathan, became president and secured the PDP presidential nomination in 2011, drawing on the power of his incumbency... Jonathan could well remain in office until 2015. In this situation, Northerners fear political marginalization, which means reduced access to the oil revenues and patronage that fuel Nigeria's political economy. The North has long feared domination by the more advanced South, and, hence, was unenthusiastic about independence. Distrust of the South remains widespread, and there is the long standing view that only through political power can the North catch up to, or even hold its own with, the South."

This view of Jonathan as an opportunist is a familiar theme, widely repeated by his critics, typically from Northern networks thwarted by Jonathan's rise, to the point that it has become an unchallenged orthodoxy among the less well informed abroad. In many ways the idea that the North is being marginalised is a short-term one, however. Since independence in 1960, Northern power-blocks, not Southern ones, have dominated Nigerian politics. "For the Southerners it was normal," says one presidential aide from the south. "They never thought about power. They had never been in power. It was normal for them that the North governed the country, it had always been so."

Regional balance has always been a delicate issue in a country as diverse as Nigeria. The constitution makes provision for the reflection of 'federal character' in key appointments, that all regions should be fairly represented, with each of Nigeria's 36 states, for example, having a Minister in the Federal Executive Council. But the constitution provides no mechanism for the rotation of power, nor does any political party. When Jonathan stood for the PDP's nomination in 2011, he stood against a single Northern candidate. Jonathan won by a margin of 2736 to 805. If there had been an unwritten agreement, as some in the party claimed, it was a view thinly shared by delegates from across the country, who gave Jonathan 78 percent of the vote.

"The facts simply are that if the PDP had wanted a Northern candidate in 2011, it was free to choose one. It did not. And the country was free to choose a Northern President in the election itself. It did not, because far more people in the North voted for Jonathan than people in the South voted for Buhari," said one well-connected international consultant.

While Nigeria's first president after independence was a Northern-born Christian Igbo, Nnamdi Azikiwe, civilian governance was short-lived. Apart from one four-year period between 1979 and 1983, Nigeria was ruled by a series of North-dominated military juntas from 1966 to 1998. From 1976 to 1979, the officer charged with running the country was Major-General Olusegun Obasanjo, a Christian Southerner, but despite his origins Obasanjo's allegiances lay firmly within the Northern military establishment at the time. Many saw him as a puppet of the North and when he became the first military leader to transfer power to a civilian regime, it was to yet another North-dominated administration under Shehu Shagari.

"During these decades of power Northern leaders have made friends all over the world, in diplomatic circles, and amongst the business elite," says one presidential advisor. "They have accepted that power belongs to these people. So the North formed alliances that still holds today." Under military rule, the perks of government were a privilege reserved for a tiny segment of the elite; even under civilian rule, Presidents from North or South, the dividends for the overwhelming majority were slender compared with the disproportionate benefits that accrued to those closest to power.

During the dictatorship of Sani Abacha (1993–1998), Obasanjo turned and spoke out against the human rights abuses of the regime and was later imprisoned for participating in an aborted coup. Following Abacha's sudden death in 1998, Obasanjo was released and, in an abrupt turnaround in fortunes, was elected as successor to the interim ruler, General Abdulsalami Abubakar, another Northerner, a year later.

"They needed someone that they thought would gaze favourably to the North," says one government insider. "They remembered his previous loyalty and thought he would be grateful for their grand gesture."

But the Obasanjo of 1999 was a very different animal from the more subservient individual who handed over power in 1979. Some political godfathers began to say that in exchange for his "get out of jail free card" Obasanjo had agreed to serve only one four-year term before giving up his post to a northern candidate. That way an increasingly restive south would be placated but power would soon be restored to its traditional custodians. It appeared briefly as if Obasanjo might face a challenge from his deputy, Atiku Abubakar, from Adamawa state in the North East. But Atiku blinked, and agreed to support Obasanjo for a second term.

Obasanjo again stood for and won the nomination for the PDP – People's Democratic Party – in 2003 and, in the subsequent presidential contest against the Northern Muslim candidate, another former military ruler, General Muhammadu Buhari, gained a decisive victory. And in an indication of what the political establishment in Nigeria was capable of when it did find common cause, a broad coalition within the PDP helped defeat plans by Obasanjo supporters of a "Third-Term Agenda", a plan to amend the constitution so that he could serve yet another four years. The PDP insisted Obasanjo stand down; in exactly the same way four years later, the same party found no issue with Jonathan's plans to contest.

Obasanjo left power in 2007 to be succeeded by Yar'Adua. As a man of the north, Yar'Adua needed a vice president from the south and the man he chose was the relatively obscure Governor of Bayelsa, Goodluck Jonathan. "They chose Jonathan partly because he appeared to be without political ambition," says one government insider. "He wasn't aggressive. He was quiet. They though he would be grateful. So he assumed his role. But they were wrong. Jonathan wasn't weak, he was strategic, and he was free and not bound to any network or vested interests. Now they say that Jonathan has cheated the North predicated upon this idea of an unwritten power-sharing rule. But they are just scared that they have lost their grip on power. Several of the party's leading members, from the Muslim North, have defected to rival outfits, accusing Jonathan of flouting the agreement. In reality they just want to become the President and Jonathan is in their way."

Underlying this apparent North-South dispute is competition for resources and influence that is far more important to political networks themselves than those they claim to represent. The North-South division is effectively a shorthand for a very complicated phenomena that involves quite a few complex ideas, which raises awkward issues of who benefits from power. For example, after all the years when Northern leaders ruled Nigeria, the region remained desperately poor, with some of the lowest human development indicators of any part of the country.

Having assumed the presidency following Yar'Adua's death in office in 2010, Jonathan's next task was to win the nomination for the election the following year. To achieve this he had to take on the might of the Northern establishment in the shape of formidable characters such as General Ibrahim Babangida, the man dubbed the 'Maradona of Politics', with a reputation as the ultimate schemer in a land of schemers, and the tremendously wealthy Atiku Abubakar, the man who had been Obasanjo's Northern vice president.

But Jonathan's victory in 2011 changed the tactics and stance of the opposition. Before the election Jonathan was lambasted for being naïve and weak. But soon afterwards he was accused of becoming cynical and dictatorial, because of his refusal to rule out the possibility that he might seek to stand for a second term (as the constitution entitled him to do). As the 2015 election approaches, the opposition appears uncertain on their line of attack and so have formed the All Progressives Congress and enlisted the support of five dissident PDP State Governors, four from the North and one from the South.

Meanwhile, the presence of an Ijaw man at State House has attracted allies from the Niger Delta to the nation's capital. "Before Jonathan was President, if you saw someone wearing the traditional Niger Delta attire in Abuja you would stop and greet that person even if you didn't know him," says a Nigerian political analyst. "It was so rare to see someone from the Delta in the capital. Abuja was for the elite and the political class. But today, if you were to stop and great every person you see with an attire from the Delta, you would spend an entire day doing nothing but greeting people. Jonathan made Abuja more colourful."

Outsiders were impressed too. Given Nigeria's image, first-time visitors to the purpose-built capital cannot fail to be taken aback by the range of well-maintained modern buildings, the sweeping boulevards and the relative lack of congestion. Edifices such as the green-domed National Assembly building, the grand national mosque and the Milennium Tower would not look out of place in any of the world's great capitals.

"When a friend of mine, who is a member of Parliament in Sierra Leone, came to see me in Abuja last time she cried," the political analyst recalled. "She cried because she asked herself when Sierra Leone will ever be like Abuja. It defies the characterisation that is often associated with Nigeria. Abuja is a big city. It is a massive construction site and much of that is private. People are investing, both Nigerians and foreigners. A 100mx100m empty plot of land in Abuja, in the city centre, can sell for $3 million dollars. Property is a leading business.

"I have been in Abuja now for six years, and I would never live anywhere else. It's a good place to be. The whole of Nigeria is in Abuja, and part of the rest of the world is there as well. Abuja is an easy going city, it doesn't go up too early in the morning, but then it doesn't go to sleep early either."

The changing demographic of the capital may alarm Northerners but people from the Delta argue that they have little to complain about given that, in the 50 years since independence, Northern soldiers and politicians have been at the helm of government for 38 years. They also point out that while the president is a Southerner, Northerners have their hands on many of the key levers of power. The Vice President, the Senate President, the Speaker of the House, the Chief Justice, the Defence Minister, the National Security Adviser, and the President of the Federal High Court, are all from the North.

"Jonathan has spent all his time as President trying to please the North," says one government insider. "They have even received more projects than in all of the South. But that's not enough, because that's not what they want. They want power."

Outside the corridors of power, however, entrepreneurs are going about their business with a bullish attitude. One man who knows more about Nigeria than most is the country's richest man Aliko Dangote. And he is certainly confident enough to invest in its future. In 2014 he committed himself to building a $9 billion oil refinery and petrochemical plant to add to his cement and food empire. Nor is he alone. Younger entrepreneurs are using the internet and mobile phone technology to change the way people buy and pay for goods, including music and films from a thriving arts industry. Foreign companies, from fashion house Ermenegildo Zegna to GE, are building stores and factories rather than just talking about Nigeria as a potential market, as happened in the past.

"There are a lot of things that are happening in Nigeria that don't necessarily appear in the press on a daily basis, and are not spoken much about," says Phillip van Niekerk. "The gap between real risk and perceived risk is very large in Nigeria. It needs to be de-coupled. The citizens of the planet Mercury, viewing the world from a commercial prism, see that if they get this right Nigeria could be poised for an unparalleled investment bonanza. I am not saying it is going to happen, but that is why people in Johannesburg, London and New York are looking too invest in Nigeria."

As education provision is extended and infrastructure is developed, productivity is increasing. Alongside this, national morale has improved to the point that, just as the people in the US talk of the "American dream", in Nigeria they talk of the "Nigerian Dream". Parents truly believe that their child can be the next Aliko Dangote. Meanwhile, Nigeria's population, which has long been seen as one of its problems is now perceived as an opportunity. Foreign investors, once so wary, now have dollar signs in their eyes as they weigh up the potential of a country of 170 million citizens with a fast-growing middle class hungry for consumer goods.

In April 2014, Nigeria overtook South Africa to become the continent's largest economy following the recalculation of its GDP. Moving up ten notches to become the world's 27th largest economy, Nigeria has now joined the burgeoning club of middle-income countries. The size of the economy is estimated at 80.3 trillion naira ($509.9 billion), 89 per cent larger than previously stated, according to Yemi Kale, Head of the Nigerian National Bureau of Statistics.

An overhaul of Nigeria's GDP calculations was long overdue. Economies grow and change structure over time, therefore it is important to frequently update the methodology for measuring GDP in order to maintain accurate estimates. In fact, most governments overhaul their GDP calculations every few years to reflect changes in output and consumption. Nigeria's national statistics had not been updated since 1990, a decade before the country's telecoms boom and the start of its passionate love affair with Nollywood, Nigeria's $300 million-a-year-movie industry. Two decades ago, the country had only one telecoms operator with around 300,000 telephone lines. Now, four operators service Nigeria's 120 million mobile-phone subscribers. Nollywood, meanwhile, is now the second-largest producer of films in the world after India, and – almost unbelievably –

ahead of the United States and is contributing 1.42 per cent of the country's economic output.

Other smaller sectors have not been ignored either. Since 2011, a team of number-crunchers has criss-crossed Nigeria, pounding the streets to capture an up-to-date picture of the enormous informal economy ranging from barbers and tailors to cyber cafes. The base year will now be recalibrated every few years, with the next recalculation scheduled for 2016-17. Although the rebased GDP does not make Nigerians better off overnight, it has an important impact on Nigeria's ability to borrow foreign money for investments in the country, as national debt levels are measured as a percentage of debt-to-GDP. Prior to the rebasing, Nigeria had a debt-to-GDP ratio for 2012 of 19 per cent. Following the rebasing it is 11 per cent. This compares favourably with heavyweights such as South Africa, which has a debt-to-GDP ratio of 39.9 per cent, and even the UK with a ratio of 84.3 per cent. As a result, Nigeria has huge scope to raise loans for investment in domestic infrastructure. Borrowing to take the debt-to-GDP ratio back to 19 per cent would provide an additional US$36 billion.

The media has been largely uninterested in reporting the significance of the rebasing, according to Ngozi Okonjo-Iweala, Nigeria's Minister of Finance, and slow to wake up to the benefits of it. If anyone is in a position to understand just how important the rebasing is, it's Okonjo-Iweala. A former managing director at the World Bank, she narrowly missed out on being appointed its president before resuming her political career in her home country at the personal request of President Jonathan after he appealed to her patriotic instincts.

"When we tried to rebase the economy, they tried to twist the story," she says, "but, fortunately, all the negative people failed. We had outside organisations to come and validate the numbers and they came and did that over a three-month period. So they were able to come out themselves, like the IMF and the World Bank, and say that the numbers were properly done. The negative people could not overcome the excitement of the Nigerians."

Granted, bigger is not always better. Although the new figures shrank the debt-to-GDP ratio, the rebasing has exposed a weaker tax base. "Our revenue-to-GDP ratio does not look that good any more," concedes Okonjo-Iweala, adding that tax collection will become a priority for the government. Nigeria's tax-to-GDP ratio in 2012 was 2.7 per cent prior to the rebasing, and 1.6 per cent after. In comparison, South Africa has a tax-to-GDP ratio of 26.4 per cent. There is therefore a huge potential to increase tax revenues, and reinvest this money in the country.

Despite strong growth and a bigger GDP, Nigeria still lags behind South Africa, the continent's only G20 member, in terms of basic infrastructure and governance. Nigeria's GDP per capita rose to $2,688 last year from an estimated $1,437 in 2012, while GDP per capita in South Africa was $7,508. Looked at on a GDP per capita basis, Nigeria's position is much more modest, ranking it 130th in the world. Still, such a low GDP per capita number suggests that the development potential for the country is immense, and could be compared to China's GDP per capita, which is 2.3 times greater than that of Nigeria.

Then there is the question of power, or the lack thereof. At 4,000 megawatts, Nigeria's electricity output is a tenth of South Africa's for a population three times the size. And it is very much front of people's minds. Ask someone outside of Nigeria what the country's "number one problem" is and they would probably say corruption. But if you ask a Nigerian, they will invariably say power, with corruption coming a relatively lowly third or even of fourth.

According to the analyst Phillip van Niekerk: "Nigeria is sometimes very bad at doing the big things, but very good at doing the small steps. I recently met with this small Nigerian company, which wants to develop compressed natural gas devices to replace the diesel generators at hotels, and residences in Lagos. Now this is a small step, but it presents the possibility of small scale power and to skirt around some of the massive infrastructure challenges that large scale electricity generation presents."

It is true that the president has a long list of problems to address – crime, corruption, lack of governance, education and a better infrastructure. But despite all of this, Nigeria remains a country that it has huge potential and is easy to get excited about.

Just weeks before the GDP overhaul the World Bank listed Nigeria among the "Extreme Poor Nations." But Jonathan responded by saying that the realities on ground did not reveal a poor nation, but a nation with abundant wealth, which needs to be more evenly redistributed. Addressing workers at the May Day rally in 2014 held at Eagle Square, Abuja, Jonathan said: "The nation is not poor. The challenge of the country is not poverty, but redistribution of wealth… Nigeria is not a poor country. Nigerians are the most travelled people. There is no country you go that you will not see Nigerians. The GDP of Nigeria is over half a trillion dollars and the economy is growing at close to 7 per cent…. Our problem is not poverty, our problem is redistribution of wealth."

Okonjo-Iweala says that her former employer, the World Bank, is one of the culprits when it comes to this area. "Instead of 66 per cent being defined as the absolute poor, they now say it is 33 per cent and it is due to poor estimation of the numbers," she says. "All along we had doubted those numbers, but you know it is so political. Here in Nigeria the atmosphere is to make people feel very badly off and like nothing is happening. And then if you tell them that the poverty numbers are wrong they just think you are playing politics. So we left it alone, we let it be an international institution to make that judgement. But when the new numbers came out, I thought I would get a lot of calls, but most of the newspapers are opposition papers you see, so nobody has called me."

She accepts that a figure of 33 per cent of the population living in poverty means that it remains a grave problem but argues that the way forward is to foster those areas of the economy which have the potential to create the most jobs.

"Nigerians don't want hand-outs," she says. "They do not have that type of mentality. They want to be entrepreneurial, they want to sell something, they want to work, they want to farm, they want something to do for themselves. So what you are looking at is what are those sectors that can create the most jobs for young people. So under this administration we have focused on agriculture in a new and modern way. Then manufacturing is another area that is growing very well. We have a large consumer market, so the focus on consumer goods is a good thing. We focus on housing. Just to name a few. And it is through those means of getting people meaningfully employed that we can create redistributive policies. Like that it does not become a huge fiscal drag on the Government and the public purse."

The "redistributive policies" to which Okonjo-Iweala refers appear to revolve around a fledgling "social protection system" she is working on. She chairs a committee set up by the President to look into ways of introducing elements of welfare to help the worst off and to promote education among the poor. Examples of this include conditional cash transfers to mothers, whereby in return for a sum of money they submit themselves to prenatal care, immunise their children and send them to school.

"We are already piloting a system in Kano," she says. "We give cash transfers to parents in order for them to send their daughters to school, and these have resulted in a 40 per cent increase in enrolment already, so we know it can work. I am really confident that we can create jobs and development all the way down to the bottom."

And travellers to Abuja can see evidence of this within minutes of touching at the capital's Nnamdi Azikiwe

International Airport. The moment each passenger clears the departure hall he or she becomes part of the vibrant local economy. Official and unofficial porters will jostle for the right to carry their bags. Taxi drivers compete for custom on the basis not just of price or boot capacity but model type, air conditioning, even cleanliness. Once on the road the crash course in small-time entrepreneurship Nigerian-style continues. Every time a car stops at traffic lights or is caught in gridlock – an occupational hazard in any Nigerian city – street sellers will appear at the window. Meanwhile, drivers of private cars find themselves subjected to the high-pressure sales tactics of windscreen cleaners. Most work on the assumption that the average ex-pat is too much of a lightweight to create a fuss if they are faced with a fait accompli and simply get to work with their squeegee. Once the job is done, it takes a hard-hearted – and courageous – driver not to make an appropriate payment.

This spirit of free enterprise does not evaporate outside the city limits of Lagos or Abuja. Instead it relentlessly continues into what can only be described as a kind of urbanised countryside. "You leave Abuja behind and the commerce continues," says Phillip van Niekerk. "After three hours it is still there, it goes on and on, it doesn't stop. Everyone is out there doing things. This is Nigeria. That's what Nigerians are really good at, they are traders."

No surprise to hear, then, that Nigeria's richest man, Aliko Dangote, has trading in his blood. His great-grandfather on his mother's side, Alhassan Dantata, was one of West Africa's richest merchants, who brought kola nuts from Ghana and exported groundnuts from Nigeria. Dantata's entrepreneurial acumen cascaded down the generations but found its most sublime exponent in Dangote.

Like his distinguished forebear, Dangote started in buying and selling but he was smart enough to spot the bigger margins to be made in manufacturing. Today he meets the essential daily food needs of nearly 600 million Africans through the manufacture of sugar, milk, noodles, macaroni, spaghetti, tomato paste, fruit juice, flour, bread and rice. His also kept a close eye on the evolution of government policy and when it became clear that the authorities were keen to switch to the manufacture of cement rather than the importation of it, he saw his chance. The French building materials giant Lafarge had a dominant position in the Nigerian cement market at this point but was unwilling to invest in manufacturing plant. By stepping into the breach Dangote turned himself into a player in that sector.

Unlike some, Dangote has made all his money in Africa, and most of it in Nigeria. Today Dangote is the largest employer not only in Nigeria but West Africa a whole. In 2008 Dangote became the first Nigerian to make it onto Forbes' rich list and three years later the magazine disclosed: "The Nigerian businessman's fortune surged 557 per cent in the past year, making him the world's biggest gainer in percentage terms and Africa's richest individual for the first time." According to Forbes – which estimates his wealth at $25 billion – he is the 43rd wealthiest person in the world and the richest person in Africa.

"The Nigerian dream is real," says Antony Goldman. "You

have Jonathan, the President of Nigeria, going from middle-ranking civil servant to President in ten years. You have Atiku Abubakar, an orphan in the North, becoming one of the richest and one of the most influential people in the country. There is a blend of people in Nigeria. There are those who get the opportunity and only see it as winning a lottery ticket. There are some people who got oil licences under Babangida and now own flats at One Hyde Park [London's most exclusive apartment block complex]. They got their licence, they farmed it out to someone, and cashed in the money.

"But there are others who see Nigeria as a platform, and they have created things. Dangote is the most obvious one, but there are probably two dozen people at the level below him, and several hundred people at the level below that. And it continues. There are lots of entrepreneurs in Nigeria. It's just about continuing to create an enabling platform for those people. Which means better access to credit, which is still not easy, and of course better access to infrastructure in all its forms."

The man himself reckons there remains huge scope for growth if the government can make the electricity network function properly. As Dangote says: "Nigeria has been growing at 7 per cent with zero power for the last decade, imagine what we can do when we get power. Then I am not going to be the richest man in Africa, I am going to be the richest man in the world."

One of the heartening aspects of Dangote's story is that his wealth has its roots away from the usual cash cows around the oil sector. While there is no doubt that he started out from a position of privilege, Dangote does not trade in oil and has never been in government. He stands out from Nigeria's super-wealthy elite because he achieved his position not by flipping contracts and securing concessions in the oil industry but by securing a dominant share of trade by proving himself in the manufacturing sector.

Another more traditional entrepreneur is Pascal Dozie, the son of a country court interpreter from Owerri in Imo State. "We did not have many modern facilities, but we had the village set up," he recalls. "If you were hungry, someone would feed you. If your neighbour caught you doing something wrong, they would punish you. When your parents found out, they would talk to the neighbour to make sure they had given you a proper spanking. Modernity has changed all of this."

When Nigeria became independent in the 1960s, Dozie was offered a scholarship by the London School of Economics and left for England. Unlike some classmates such as Mick Jagger – who dropped out to form the Rolling Stones – Dozie left with a degree and a certain amount of work experience. Back in Lagos, he set up his own consultancy, the African Development Consulting Group, and has not worked for anyone else since.

The business prospered on the back of projects for blue-chip names such as Nestle and Pfizer and then Dozie had his big idea. He remembered from his childhood the difficulties that Nigerian traders from the remote villages in the east of the country faced in keeping secure the big bundles of cash they carried to and from Lagos for business. "Sometimes they would be waylaid by rogues on the road," he says. Life would be so much less stressful if they could wire their cash ahead. So, Dozie pioneered electronic money transfers in Nigeria.

It was on the back of the popularity of this service that Dozie set up Diamond Bank in 1991. "The first customer was my wife," laughs Dozie. "The assumption was we were going to come by money easily – it wasn't easy." The problem was that most companies at that time would not deal with a bank less than three years old. The only way to make it work was for Dozie's small but dedicated team to make personal visits to potential customers – from traders to car dealers – and persuade them to part with their money so that the bank could build its capital reserves through their deposits.

The big break that made him seriously rich came when the South African mobile company, MTN, approached Dozie with the idea of setting up a cell phone network in the vast and unexplored Nigerian market. Many people who had observed the struggles of the government telecoms company, NITEL, were sceptical. Investors said that if the state could not set up a cell phone network, no one could. But they were wrong. "Most of the people I asked to invest now regret not investing – I even regret it myself," says Dozie. "They would have enjoyed returns of 20 times their money." Dozie is now worth in the region of US$1.1 billion, according to Forbes.

Another Nigerian on Forbes' list is Tony Elemelu. A trained economist, Elumelu made his first impact on Nigeria's financial services industry in 1997 when he led a small group of investors in the take-over of a distressed medium-sized commercial bank in Lagos. It was subsequently renamed Standard Trust Bank and the following year Elumelu was appointed its Chief Executive Officer. He was only 34 at the time, the youngest CEO of a commercial bank in Nigeria. His lack of experience proved no barrier to success and he went on to turn Standard Trust into a top-five player in Nigeria's banking sector. In 2005, Elumelu's corporate reputation was sealed when he pulled off the largest merger in the history of the banking sector in Sub-Saharan Africa with the acquisition of United Bank of Africa, then the country's third biggest bank. The new entity took the name of the larger partner, United Bank of Africa, and Elumelu was installed as Chief Executive.

Elumelu went on to coin the term "Africapitalism" which he defines as an "economic philosophy that embodies the African private sector's commitment to the economic transformation of Africa through long-term investments that create economic prosperity and social wealth." He is now one of Africa's most sought-after business speakers, and his ideas on Africapitalism have featured prominently in shaping Nigeria's growth story.

But it is the rise of an emerging and assertive middle class that will prove more significant in the medium and long term. This segment of society has seen unparalleled growth over the past decade. Until 2000, Nigeria was run by a tiny elite that was unaccountable and self-interested, while at the bottom an enormous underclass struggled to get by. In between the two was a "squeezed middle" of civil servants and lawyers. In this context, people like Peter Lewis have identified a "lack of opportunity" for ordinary Nigerians, but times have changed.

"If you visited someone in Nigeria who lived in a one-bedroom apartment in Diobu (a poor neighbourhood in Port Harcourt) two years ago and then returned today there is a good chance he will have moved," says a Nigerian journalist. "Now he may well live in Government Reserved Area (the wealthy area in Port Harcourt). That's the possibilities in Nigeria. That's Nigeria today. Jonathan made this journey."

A company that comes to Africa wanting to invest often divides the population according to five income categories: A, B, C, D, and E. The As are the very rich. The Bs, Cs and the Ds are what can be referred to as "Africa 2", and it is among these consumers that these companies find their target audiences and see the opportunities. It is estimated that more than 40 per cent of the Nigerian population, almost 70 million people, have now moved into "Africa 2". They are not middle class as perceived by the West. They don't have swimming pools, nice houses and a Volvo. But in Nigerian terms they are, and there are now a vast number of people in that category. People with a disposable income, who increasingly pay taxes, and do not feel intimidated by the state. They earn their keep by themselves.

When it comes to population, Nigeria has what is known as good "inner" demographics. That is to say it has a very youthful population and so we are going to see a rise in the number of people eligible to work relative to those not working. This means that if productivity targets are hit, Nigeria will not have to wrestle with the problem of supporting the elderly, which so many countries in the old world are currently struggling with. Instead Nigeria is being driven by a new generation of young entrepreneurs, many of them educated overseas. Then, unlike many Africans, who see foreign study as a chance to migrate for good, Nigerians are willing to travel abroad to gain a degree and then return to Nigeria to invest and build. They do not rely on state patronage any more. They are people who see themselves as "businessmen and women" like anywhere else in the world. Nigeria is changing before our eyes, but often only the chaos makes the headlines. The Nigerian success story is too often forgotten, or simply ignored.

"Nigeria is on its way of becoming a banking and financial services nation," says Phillip van Niekerk. "The country in the process of overcoming the curse of its oil bounty – one of the main impediments to Nigeria's development over the last 50 years," he adds.

"Nigeria's future lies not in oil and gas but in non-oil sectors such as agriculture, housing, creative arts and services, which account for more than 80 per cent of GDP," said Okonjo-Iweala. "For sustainable growth and development, we must build enduring institutions in these sectors. We must fight corruption and we must ensure that as our country develops it also becomes more transparent."

Okonjo–Iweala has played her own significant part in the drive towards transparency. Innovations she introduced during her first term as Finance Minister from 2003 to 2006, appear to be bearing fruit. One of these is the Excess Crude Account, a mechanism for managing the volatility of government revenues. The Finance Ministry sets a benchmark oil price and when the price rises above this all supplementary revenues are saved. The resulting fund is then used to cushion expenditure when the price falls.

She also put in place new accounting systems: the

Integrated Personnel and Payroll Information System (IPPIS), the Government Integrated Finance Management System (GIFMS), and the Treasury Single Account System (TSAS).

The IPPIS means that every single government worker is now paid electronically from a central government fund rather than manually by their respective departments as was the case previously. The old system resulted in widespread corruption, with officials taking a cut of monies paid out, and in some instances people would not be paid at all.

The GIFMS enables the Treasury and all the other departmental offices to talk to each other using an electronic system that is transparent. Under the old manual system they were forced to consult a central authority to find out their departmental account balances but now it is just a matter of checking their computer.

The TSAS allows the Minister of Finance to get an overview of all the money in the system. If budgets are being stretched, the minister can work out who is running a surplus and transfer funds to where money is more tight. "[This means] you don't overspend your overdraft with the Central Bank," says Okonjo-Iweala. "It is a very important tool and it also brings more transparency."

She adds: "It is very pleasing to me that I have come back and see that those fundamental systems I built are still in place and working. My strong belief is that Nigeria is really going to emerge as a very strong economy in the world. I want Nigeria to take the place that it deserves, and not having an image where the first thing people think is 'corruption' because 99 per cent of Nigerians are not corrupt."

Her optimism is shared by Jim O'Neill, the former chief economist of Goldman Sachs, who coined the acronym BRIC in 2001 as shorthand for Brazil, Russia, India and China, the countries he predicted would come to dominate the world economy. Nigeria no longer needs to look elsewhere for an economic model on which to base its development, he says. Instead it should look to its young entrepreneurs. "The most exciting thing about Nigeria is its people, says O'Neill: "It's a place where making money is in the blood."

Indeed, he has such faith in Nigeria that when he came to anoint his latest quartet of outperformers in 2014 for a series on BBC radio he included it in his line-up. The MINT group of countries, distinguished by their fast economic growth and large, young populations, are Mexico, Indonesia, Nigeria, and Turkey.

"The BRIC and the MINT countries, if I'm right, over the next decade will... shape the world economy's development," O'Neill told reporters on the sidelines of an Africa Finance Corporation conference in Lagos. "And if that's the case, they will be the most successful places in terms of investments too."

And O'Neill is not the only cheerleader for Nigeria. In his book "Breakout Nations: In Pursuit of the Next Economic Miracles," Ruchir Sharma, head of emerging markets at Morgan Stanley, refers to Nigeria as the "next economic star". He added, there "is more to the Nigerian economy than oil. Although the country has been infamous for its corrupt regimes, President Goodluck Jonathan looks to be targeting all the right steps to unleash growth."

Despite the growing evidence of economic progress, the international media persists in characterising Nigeria as a country where the majority of the population live in abject poverty, often citing an income of less than US$2 a day. Fortunately, South African mobile phone company MTN refused to believe figures such as this when it entered the Nigerian market a decade ago. Its success exploded the myth that the country was too poor and unstable to be worth investing in and blazed a trail for other service industries to profit from Nigeria's emergence from stagnation and conflict.

Today there are more than 70 million mobile phone subscribers in Nigeria. MTN has more customers, and makes more money in Nigeria than it does in its native South Africa. And the inter-connect between mobile phones and banking, which is already being exploited, is just the beginning of another revolution that could result in the construction of a bridge for the vast amount of capital in the informal sector – a previously cash-based economy – to move in and out of the formal economy.

Nigeria's growth is increasingly being driven by the non-oil economy. The boom in organised retail, led by chains such as Shoprite, Checkers and Massmart (which have been acquired by the US supermarket giant Walmart), is a good example. Dozens of shopping malls are being built in cities up and down the country as Nigeria's new middle class celebrates the rise in its disposable income. Everywhere you turn there are fresh developments and new projects funded by private-sector operators.

A good example of this is the privatisation of the fertiliser business. The government is determined to reduce the company's dependence on imports and set itself a deadline of 2015 for the disposal of its assets in this sector. The first step was taken as early as 2006, when Indorama acquired Eleme Petrochemicals Company, a subsidiary of Nigerian National Petroleum Corporation (NNPC), for US$400 million. It is now engaged in the construction of a US$1.8 billion fertiliser methanol plant on a greenfield site in Port Harcourt, the largest project of its kind in Nigeria, as part of its plan to create the largest petrochemicals hub in the country.

This is a highly significant move in a country where the agricultural sector still employs around 70 per cent of the population. By supplanting expensive imported fertiliser with cheaper domestically manufactured product from Eleme farmers are expected to generate higher yields.

Exploratory mining exploration has also come back on a scale that has not been seen since the 1970s. Though largely unscoped, Nigeria has meaningful reserves of iron ore, gold, and coal, as well as industrial minerals such as bitumen, limestone and clay. According to the Minister of Mines and Steel Development, Musa Sada, the mining industry is set to pick up some of the slack from the oil sector, contributing 5 per cent of GDP by 2020, up from a current level of less than 1 per cent. "Our position is to make sure that there is some kind of diversification," says Sada.

Indeed Nigeria is already exporting iron ore with the help of a newly completed railroad that takes the ore from Itakpe to Warri. This stretch of railway had been in the planning since the "3rd National Plan" of 1975, primarily to serve the country's steel industry. These plans were subsequently abandoned, restarted, and then abandoned again until Jonathan's administration finally completed the project in December 2013.

As Africa's most populous nation, with a population of 170 million people, Nigeria should be a magnet for foreign investment. The fact remains, however, that it is a country with inherited colonial borders, an estimated 400 ethnic and linguistic groups, 80 million Muslims, and another 80 million Christians. In such a context compromise is inevitable. Many point to the popular protests that forced the government to do a u-turn on its plan to revoke the fuel subsidy in 2012 as a Nigerian version of the Arab Spring. Such an interpretation misses one vital point. Unlike the Middle Eastern regimes that were overturned by people power, Nigeria is not an autocracy run by a despot. It is a democracy with an elected government and one of the most free presses in Africa, which attacks the President in public on a daily basis. Dysfunctional it may be but dictatorial it is not.

In time, we may well come to see the fuel subsidy episode as a sign of the maturing of Nigeria as a democracy rather than the opposite. The people who took to the streets had a very clear understanding of what was at stake. The very elite that was responsible for corruption and government waste wanted to continue to share out the spoils of the country's wealth among themselves while at the same time depriving the have-nots of one of the few benefits the system afforded them: subsidised fuel.

The popular outrage arose from a refusal to take more pain while the slicing and dicing of the patronage machine continued and a determination to hold the administration and its courtiers accountable. This amounts to evidence of the growing economic and political empowerment of a substantial section of the community. As such, the scale of the protests can be seen as evidence of how far Nigeria has come over the last decade.

Even in the febrile environment of a hotly contested State election in Osun in 2014, there were signs of a shift in Nigeria's political culture. At a campaign rally in Osogbo in July, people seen waving ballot cards, just one indication of a more open and democratic spirit, a process more about the bottom up than the top down. The incumbent Governor of Osun, felt the pressure of a genuinely open political contest. "The Governor owed civil servants two months of salary, and he went around to see how he could pay them, because he knew that if he did not pay their salary they would not vote for him in the elections", said Jonathan. "And in these elections you could no longer force yourself to victory, you could not fake the ballots and manipulate the system any more. So to win the elections people must vote for you, and for them to vote for you, you must do what is right. You cannot not pay your workers and expect to win elections, and so he immediately found money to pay his workers. He was not threatened by anyone. It is a small step in a big country, but it is a very important victory"

Democracy in action rather than mindless thuggery. It may be time for the Plutonians to become Mercunauts.

Chapter Four

THE GOD THAT SUCCEEDED

One of the most depressing facts about Nigeria's recent history is that the political parties contesting the first elections after independence made the provision of a reliable supply of electric power a cornerstone of their manifestos. And that very same promise – unfulfilled to this day – remains one of the most potent electoral issues. Indeed, the issue has become such a standing joke that government bodies with responsibilities in this area became national laughing stocks. Hence the Power Holding Company of Nigeria (PHCN) was rechristened "Please Have Candles Nearby" by disgruntled consumers and its predecessor, the National Electrical Power Authority (NEPA), was known as "Never Expect Power Always".

The Nigerian President who does eventually get to grips with the power issue can expect a host of dividends. Apart from making the electors happy, he or she can expect a significant boost in terms of economic growth in areas such as manufacturing and agriculture. President Jonathan recognises this and has made a series of bold moves to address the problem that in 2013 culminated in Africa's biggest ever privatisation.

However, wholesale reform and large-scale investment is required in the infrastructure of all three key sectors of the Nigerian economy. Apart from power generation and distribution, transport and agriculture both require radical change. Privatisation has been selected as the agent of this change in all three areas. Here we look at the state of each ailing sector in turn and the measures being taken to cure the patient.

POWER

The Nigerian government accepts that access to electricity can be a game-changer. If capacity can be increased on a meaningful scale, several percentage points could be added to GDP growth and manufacturing and agriculture will be stimulated.

If you are new to Nigeria, the power situation takes a little getting used to. There are frequent and often night-long power cuts with the result that anyone who can afford one invests in a back-up generator that is switched on when the national grid goes down. People dash out in the pouring rain and pitch dark with a torch to try to crank up the generator and from those who have been careless enough to let their stock of petrol or diesel run too low, the mournful cry can be heard of "Fuel no dey!", pidgin for "No fuel!".

During the tumultuous years of the Abacha regime in the 1990s there was no investment in this sector, at all. And when Jonathan came to power almost two-thirds of all electricity in Nigeria was produced by generators humming in basements and backyards across the country, despite the allocation of more than USD20 billion to the sector by his two predecessors. Not surprisingly, ordinary Nigerians were angry at being restricted to a few hours of electricity per day. One presidential aide recalls a particularly galling episode while watching a football match. "It's much better now," he says. "But I remember when I was watching the 2004 African Nations Cup in Tunisia, Nigeria was playing against Cameroon. Jay Jay Okocha was putting on a show. He is a master dribbler, he controls the ball. He is a fantastic footballer. Anyway, he was running towards the goal, and the power went off. Afterwards I heard he scored four times! I missed all of them. That is maybe not a tragedy, but if a child is reading for an exam and the power goes off, he has to stop. You need your own generator, which is very expensive."

The truth is that the Nigerian power sector has been in crisis for decades. Much of the generation, transmission and distribution hardware has become worn out or damaged. When Jonathan took office, Nigeria's average annual per capita power consumption was among the lowest in the world, an extraordinary state of affairs in a country that is the world's fifth largest oil producer. In 2010 Nigeria's per capita electricity consumption was 7 per cent of Brazil's and 3 per cent of South Africa's. At the same time, at least 50 per cent of Nigerian households were not connected to the national grid and self-generation (by diesel or petrol generators) was estimated to amount to 6,000MW. Jonathan himself comes from a state where the federal government had not installed any power cables until December 2005. In fact, up to that date it had provided no electrical supply of any kind in the whole of Bayelsa state. Instead the authorities were using their own turbines, installed during the Second Republic when Chief Melford Okilo was the Governor of the old River State.

It was President Obasanjo who started the process of improving the investment in power. But the project was plagued by delays and mismanagement, and allegations that public funds were being diverted by well-connected but unscrupulous contractors. The programme failed to make much of an impact. "When [Umaru] Yar'Adua became President the previous government, under Obasanjo, had already injected over US$20 billion into the power sector to build gas-powered electricity plants," says a Nigerian political analyst. "Not much had come out of it so Yar'Adua suspended the process to see what had gone wrong, what had been done, or what hadn't been done. But then two years passed and nothing was moving forward, nothing at all. Under Yar'Adua there was a fear of losing control of the power sector. There were those in the Yar'Adua entourage who thought that government should always run the business, that people in power would always have the opportunity to make money out of it. That's why they were against the power privatisations all together. Then when it came to the Independent Power Projects (IPPs) they wanted to cancel them so that they could reward them to themselves, simple as that."

When Jonathan first took office the privatisation programme had ground to a halt due to a two-year investigation into alleged corruption surrounding the award of several contracts and Nigerians were still without power for much of the time. The new president got the privatisation process back on track by the simple expedient of appointing himself Minister of Power. In April 2010, Jonathan set up a "war cabinet", including the Finance Minister, to address the issue and scheduled "weekly power meetings" at 11am on Tuesdays.

The first issue on the agenda was the rehabilitation of under-performing assets, which had not been adequately maintained for decades. This was done by adding more generating and transmission capacity to the grid, as well as stabilising the network by reducing the alarming number of system collapses. The ambitious programme launched to confront this was the Power Sector Reform Roadmap. And there are signs that it has been a success. Today, the national grid generates a little over 4,000MW of electricity, up from 2,300MW in 2010.

"Jonathan started the implementation of the power road map, and it has been successful," says one aide. "Even more important is that it has been transparent. There was a process that was followed and adhered to. We now know that the power sector will improve. If the buyers do not manage it and improve it, they will lose it. This is Jonathan's signature achievement. The closest thing to any allegations of corruption was Bart Nnaji, the Energy Minister, who had interests in one of the generation companies which he did not fully disclose and was therefore forced to resign. That was really unfortunate, because he was an excellent minister. But the process was implemented."

Jonathan's strategy has been a qualified success, but it remains early days. Much still remains to be done. An output of 4,000MW is totally inadequate to supply the needs of a population of 170 million. In contrast, Brazil generates 100,000MW of grid-based power for its 201 million citizens and South Africa generates 40,000MW for 50 million.

The gains achieved so far have bought some breathing space for the major reforms that are required to attract the investment needed to give Nigerian consumers and businesses the power they so desperately need. But in the government's view, this will only be achieved when Africa's biggest ever privatisation has been completed.

The first stage has already been implemented. PHCN, the Power Holding Company of Nigeria, despite the fun made of its acronym, has successfully, and transparently been unbundled and privatised into six generation and 11 distribution companies. A licensing process has also been completed to facilitate the privatisation of 34 Independent Power Projects (IPP).

The Government has entered into MOUs with world-leading companies in the power sector, such as General Electric, Siemens, Daewo and Electrobras, to invest significant equity in various power projects that will, in the end, add thousands of megawatts of capacity.

The American Exim bank has signed an MOU with the Government to provide an investment window of up to US$1.5 billion for investors looking to invest in the Nigerian power sector. This is the first time in the bank's history that it has made available such a significant amount for one specific sector in Africa.

"If Jonathan is allowed to continue what he started, a realistic timeframe is two years," says one power sector analyst.

"They need to deal with the gas issue for the generation side, and a network renewal. But then in two years time we will have a relatively stable power supply. After that we will have a power supply that can drive development. That is an incredible achievement for a man who started with nothing in a country of 170 million people, to give them power."

When Jonathan was asked about the reforms in the power sector during his first press conference, on June 20, 2010, he replied: "The power issue is almost like a chain that has so many weak links... People come to say that they want to install gas turbines... So many turbines were imported. But at the time the turbines were being imported, they did not really look at transmission infrastructure, even where you will install the turbines. There were so many things that were not properly examined... It is now we realise that even if you install all of those turbines, and all of them are generating power, you can't even transmit. So, many other transmission projects have now been awarded. These projects are ongoing. There are not projects that you can complete overnight.

"And so I tell people whenever they comment about power infrastructure, that power is different from roads. For roads, immediately you clear the area, some categories of vehicles will begin to use the road. You stabilise it. You put crushed rocks, or hard-core, some other categories will begin to use. It is just that it will be dusty before you put the asphalt. But for power, before you complete the tiniest nut, the bulb will not glow. So, I will say that our plan for Nigeria to have stable power is to really complete the reform in the power sector. The idea is that if in other countries around us, the private sector is playing a big role, why not Nigeria? Because the feeling that the government will do everything is another thing that is impoverishing Nigeria. Because even the things the private sector could have done, we are spending more money because we are waiting for the government to do everything."

The president's analysis is echoed by Dr Samuel Amadi, Chairman of the Nigerian Electricity Regulatory Commission, who memorably describes the mismatch between the scale of generating power now in place and the inadequacy of the network available to distribute it as like having "a Ferrari engine in a Volvo". According to Amadi:

"After the privatisation of PHCN we now have the power plants, we have the mega structure. What we need now is the infrastructure... We need to address the network, and we are. That is the next step. Then, any final success is dependent on the gas reforms currently lacking. So we have the power plants but no gas. It is a complicated matrix where we need all components in order for it to work. Before we were missing all of them. Now we have built the foundation and it is time for the next step. What we have done in only four years is quite unheard of, unfortunately it doesn't make for a catchy headline. But wait and see. We will get there, headlines or no headlines. We will get the job done, just give us some time."

In April 2012, in a bid to make the power sector more attractive to outside investors, electricity tariffs were increased. At the time, Nigeria was selling power below cost at an average of about 10 naira, or just six US cents, per kilowatt-hour, one of the cheapest rates in Africa. The decision was controversial, nevertheless, coming as it did just a month after the removal of fuel subsidies, which prompted street protests and a week-long nationwide strike. Jonathan's administration responded by saying that the higher "cost-reflective tariffs" for residential and commercial electricity customers were necessary to ensure that investors could make a profit. Under the new pricing regime, tariffs would rise by 25-88 per cent, though most customer classes would see a 50 per cent increase in their bills.

The government also sought to cushion the blow for the poorest consumers – something it did not do after removing the fuel subsidy – by implementing a "lifeline tariff" of four naira per kilowatt-hour for those consuming below 50 kilowatt-hours per month. In 2012, this subsidy cost the government 60 billion naira. "We are making sure that the urban poor and rural dwellers be provided a subsidy so that they don't see a significant increase in tariff," said Bart Nnaji, the Minister of Power. "The rest should be able to pay for it."[1]

The new tariff was calculated to reflect the real cost of supplying electricity, with a return on investment factored in, according to the Electricity Regulatory Commission. This comes to about 23 naira per kilowatt-hour, which is close to the average price in Africa and less than half the cost of self-generated power in Nigeria. However, politically this presents a delicate challenge to balance.

Under the new rates, the biggest consumers of electricity, wealthy individuals and businesses, pay the highest bills, cross-subsidising the less well-off. As Jonathan said in June 2014: "It is not as if we were not paying. What is being done is to adjust to make the low-income people who just use power for lighting, for radio, maybe for refrigerator and television, to pay lower than what you were paying before. But the commercial houses, industrial houses and major business outfits would pay a little more. ... What we are doing in the tariffs is to make sure that those who can afford pay, but those whose incomes are very low, pay very little. ... But the basic thing is that those who are low down should pay less than what they are even paying before, but those who can afford pay higher so that you encourage the private sector to come in. And until the private sector come in, you will not get the power you are talking about."

With a proper pricing regime in place, coupled with a sound regulatory framework, Amadi reckons the stage is set for large scale private investment but stresses the need for patience in the short term: "We now have a market that is attractive for investors with reforms that have been locked into laws with an independent regulator. It is starting to become financially viable. But it is important to appreciate that this is a transition. We have made a first foot print but there is still a long way to go. People ask, 'Why there is no power?' I answer that first of all there is power, but yes we need more power. But we started from nothing, we need a little patience to build it up. Nigeria is a vast country in geographical mass, and even greater in cultural variety with over 170 million people. You can't believe that we can have a completely integrated system up and running over night? Tell me one country which achieved that? Why should we be judged any differently?

TRANSPORT

Just next to the main ticket booth at Lagos train station, a faded, water-stained and torn list of rules and regulations governing the railway sat behind two glass frames, as recently as 2011. The laws had not been altered since their passage in 1956, four years before Nigeria became an independent nation. Even the fine amounts were listed in British pounds. These vintage regulations showed just how little had changed about Nigeria's railway system since the British opened the nation's first train track between its colonial headquarters in Lagos and Ibadan 90 miles (140km) to the north in 1900.

In 1912 a much longer route was launched to the northern city of Kano, then a hub of groundnut production. However, back in 1912 rather than moving people, the British-run railway network focused on the lucrative transportation of commodities to turn a good and quick profit for the empire. Annual exports of peanuts, for example, jumped from roughly 1,000 tons to around 41,000 tons in a mere five years thanks to the impact of the new railroad. By the time the British left in the 1960s, Nigeria had more than 2,200 miles (3,500km) of railway track criss-crossing the country.

Half a century later little has changed. On paper the Nigerian Railway Corporation still records the same amount of railroad. However, in reality the majority of the track has simply disintegrated after years of neglect. Rain has washed away bridges and culverts, while the tropical climate of Lagos has rusted the rails, and the sand corroded the tracks in the North. Indeed, Adeseyi Sijuwade, the managing director of the state-run Nigerian Railway Corporation, recently estimated that as much of 70 per cent of the track on the Lagos-to-Kano line simply does not exist anymore. So chaotic was the administration of the rail system that as coup followed coup some employees died while waiting for retirement benefits that went unpaid.

Periodic attempts were made to revive it. President Shehu Shagari, who was deposed by the military in 1983, was the first in a long line of leaders that included military rulers Muhammadu Buhari, Ibrahim Babangida and Sani Abacha, and former elected President Olusegun Obasanjo, to promise improvements. Successive governments brought in Romanians, Indians and later the Chinese to manage the promised revamp. But a combination of government inertia and failing lines, meant the trains disappeared. It is safe to say that when Jonathan came to power few people under the age of 25 had never travelled on a Nigerian train. As Sijuwade says: "The Nigerian railway system has been moribund for decades."

But under the current president the railway system is undergoing a quiet renaissance. New train lines from Lagos to Kano, Port Harcourt to Maiduguri, and Itakpi to Warri, have been built since 2011. In Lagos, formerly the world's only mega-city without an urban rail system, work has started on the first of two lines which will cost US$3.8 billion and eventually connect the four corners of the city. In Abuja, a light railway connecting the airport and satellite towns with the nation's capital is scheduled to open in 2015. This latter project, first mooted in 2006, is particularly timely as it will provide an affordable way for the city's workers to travel from the commuter towns surrounding Abuja. As a result of the rapid growth of the purpose-built capital city the stock of housing in the centre is neither sufficient for the workforce, nor affordable, forcing many to endure long commutes using a combination of the city's new bus service, and informal transport from bus terminals.

These initiatives followed the revival of the Lagos to Kano long-distance rail link, the first operational rail route in the country since the late 1980s. It is proving to be a valuable aid in easing congestion and boosting trade between the two largest cities in the country. Since it reopened, the twice-weekly route has been nearly fully booked, with passengers attracted by the low prices – at US$12, a second-class ticket is less than half the cost of the cheapest bus fare – and the relative comfort and safety of long-distance rail travel. The 1,126 km route provides a regular and safe method of transferring people and goods, as well as acting as a symbolic tie between the southern and northern halves of the country.

The resumption of the Lagos-Kano service is the first major achievement of a multibillion-dollar effort to revive Nigeria's railways. With Chinese contractors leading the way, the colonial-era network is being rehabilitated and new lines built. "Our railways have been comatose for some time," said Niyi Alli, the director of operations at the Nigerian Railway Corporation. "This is the beginning of their re-emergence."[2] Work is also underway to rehabilitate stretches of the disused railway line between Port Harcourt and Maiduguri in the North, as well as ambitious plans to eventually provide a link to the neighbouring nations of Niger and Cameroon.

Infrastructure upgrades are also under way at Nigeria's 22 airports. Some are already finished and in use, while others are at various stages of completion. Five new international terminals are also planned for Lagos, Abuja, Kano, Port Harcourt and Enugu. "All airports in Nigeria are being remodelled, many are completely new," says one presidential aide. "Stella Oduah [the former aviation minister, dismissed due to charges of corruption] was fantastic, but was forced out because of the story of the BMWs. She claimed that they were necessary to move VIPs from the airport to the city. But the truth is she just liked big cars. But the good work she did should not be taken down because of it. She was the best Aviation Minister that Nigeria has ever had. Jonathan didn't respond to the public outcry. Instead he let the institutions do their job. He doesn't want Ministers to be constantly looking over their shoulders, afraid that someone should whisper something to the President. No, he wants them to focus on their jobs."

It is the same story when it comes to Nigeria's road network. In 2013 alone, 2,000km of roads were completed, an unprecedented accomplishment in Nigeria. Most noteworthy is the Lagos to Benin road, which had been so badly maintained over the last 20 years that it was impossible to complete a round trip in a day. Now the journey takes two hours, and millions of Nigerians use the new road every year. Then there is the Lagos to Ibadan road, the busiest in West

Africa. Again, after being allowed to fall into decay over the last ten years it is now being reconstructed and expanded. The Abuja to Lokoja road, which was one of the most dangerous routes in the country, has also been rebuilt.

In a country where around 63 per cent of the population is under 25, and unemployment stands at 24 per cent, with youth unemployment at about 37 per cent, better infrastructure, more jobs, and innovative ways to pay for both are needed to ensure Nigeria's development. According to the Finance Minister, Ngozi Okonjo-Iweala, this means more public-private partnerships and it is up to the government to create "enabling environments" to attract investors. "We have embarked on a comprehensive privatisation programme in our power sector and are investing some of our petroleum subsidy savings in building roads and bridges, and improving our rail transport system," she says.

AGRICULTURE

When Nigeria gained its independence in 1960, it was an agricultural powerhouse. Not only was it the world's biggest exporter of peanuts and palm oil but also grew enough rice to feed itself with enough left over to fuel an export trade across West Africa. But, as we have seen, petroleum had just been discovered and when the oil boom started, farming was quickly forgotten. Today, not only have agricultural exports dwindled but Nigeria is one of the world's top three importers of rice, spending billions of dollars a year buying it in from as far away as Thailand. Akinwumi Adesina, Nigeria's US-educated Agriculture Minister, says: "Nigeria was food self-sufficient in the 1960s and well-known for its global position in major agricultural commodities." Then something changed, he told an audience in New York recently: "We found oil and became too dependent on it. Nigeria soon [became a net food importer, spending] on average US$11 billion on wheat, rice, sugar and fish alone."[3]

Although agriculture still accounts for more than 40 per cent of gross domestic product and is the country's biggest employer, most farms are small and yields are low. Per capita growth in production has been declining for a decade and transforming agriculture – which employs more than 50 per cent of the labour force in Nigeria – from a subsistence activity into a commercial operation is vital to reducing poverty, according to a recent IMF report.[4]

The potential is certainly there. Only about half of Nigeria's 75 million hectares of arable land is used, despite the fact that the climate is suitable for many types of crops, including rice. "We have all this potential," says Adesina. "But you can't eat potential".[5] So in 2011 the Agriculture Transformation Agenda (ATA) was launched. Critics say the activities of the ATA "produce more headlines than big crops." But Adesina is undeterred, insisting that the transformation agenda is proving effective: boosting farm output across the country, attracting millions of dollars in investment and creating badly needed jobs in rural areas. "Agriculture should be our next oil," he says. "The future of billionaires in Nigeria is in agriculture. The mistake [in the past] was to see agriculture as a development sector, not as a sector to generate wealth. Now, we look at agriculture as a business".[6]

The ATA has focused on four main areas: infrastructure to improve market access – including the building of roads and warehouses; an agricultural insurance scheme to maintain incomes if crops are damaged by bad weather; a privately managed fertiliser subsidy scheme for poor farmers; and increased import tariffs. Adesina aims to create an ecosystem in which small, medium, and large-scale farming not only coexist but flourish. "We are focusing on creating value-added products from staple crops through an aggressive import substitution programme," he says.

The creation of so-called Staple Crop Processing Zones – vast agricultural zones where food processing plants are set up to process crops into finished products for the local market – is a cornerstone of the ATA. These have already attracted strong interest from investors, including wealthy indigenous operators, drawn by the promise of a 30 per cent reduction in costs thanks to upgrades to roads, power and water. One such zone is the US$50 million farm developed by Olam, the Singapore-based commodities trading house, which is scheduled to reach 6,000 hectares by the end of the decade. On a visit to the farm in April 2014 Adesina said: "Today, is one of my happiest days as a Minister of Agriculture because of what I have seen here. The farm has the capacity to create more jobs. This single farm has employed 950 workers already and also has the capacity to produce 72,000 tonnes of paddy rice, which tells you that Nigeria can emerge as the Thailand of Africa."

He added: "I have, therefore, declared that this farm

becomes one of our staple crops processing zones and we will
partner with other development partners to build infrastructure
to attract bigger investment. The infrastructure development
will benefit the community and people around the farm and
other potential investors too."[7] The number of Staple Crop
Processing Zones in the country – including Olam Farm – has
reached 15 since 2011 and Dominion Farms, a US-based
company, has plans for an even larger rice farm.

Adesina claims that the ATA has boosted GDP by no less
than 340 billion naira and production of dry-season rice in
northern Nigeria rose to a record in 2013 after the
introduction of better seeds. This means, he says, that the
Federal Government's "revolutionary step" of attaining self-
sufficiency in rice by 2015 is now attainable. One of the more
controversial tools being used to boost the domestic
agricultural production is higher tariffs on imported rice and
wheat. The US Department of Agriculture has warned that
the import substitution policy is "weakening food security
and increasing informal cross-border trade flows in grain".

Agricultural commodities traders say there has been a
surge in imports to neighbouring Benin and Cameroon, a
sign that smuggling in to Nigeria is picking up. And the
International Monetary Fund is also encouraging Nigeria to
change its approach, saying that Abuja "should use domestic
tools that boost agricultural productivity rather than
protectionist measures".

Nigeria can nevertheless claim some success in that its
reform efforts are starting to have a positive impact.
Agricultural production has increased, and so have exports of

agricultural commodities, including cocoa, natural gum arabica, cashews, cotton and frozen shrimps. The reforms are also helping to improve the distribution of seeds and fertilisers through the use of biometric identity cards.

Credit is also flowing. The central bank is trying to increase bank lending to farmers by guaranteeing part of the debt. "The key is to get a lot more finance into the agriculture sector," says Adesina. "[Before the agenda was launched,] only 0.7 per cent of total bank lending went to the agricultural sector. Today, 5 per cent is going to farming, and [the amount is] expected to rise to 10 per cent by the end of next year." The fertiliser scheme, which relies heavily on mobile payment technology, has also won international praise. Ngozi Okonjo-Iweala, the Finance Minister, says that 90 per cent of the country's small farmers are now obtaining fertiliser, as opposed to 11 per cent before.

There are of course still enormous challenges facing Nigeria's agriculture sector. Notably, a lack of infrastructure – including roads, storage and power supply – and the insecurity generated by attacks by Boko Haram in the grain-producing states of the North East. However, significant progress is still being made.

- More than 250,000 farmers and youths in the northern states are now engaged in farming

- The first ever Nigerian database of farmers has been developed, with 6 million farmers registered and annual updates in place

- Nigeria is the first African country to have developed an e-wallet for input delivery to farmers, effectively cutting out the middle man. Private-sector seed and fertilizer companies are now selling directly to farmers via the e-wallet system

- New policies have led to the establishment of 13 new rice mills by private investors

- The Bank of Industry has signed an agreement with six tractor companies for the local production of agricultural vehicles

- The Nigerian Mortgage refinancing Company, a PPP arrangement, has been set up to enable up to 200,000 affordable mortgages within the last five years

- The Government launched a self-employment initiative under the Youth Employment In Agriculture Programme, commonly called the "Nagropreneur Programme", in 2012. This initiative, designed to encourage youth to go into commercial agriculture as entrepreneurs, is expected to have developed 750,000 young Nagropreneurs by 2015.

These statistics may sound rather dry taken individually but, if they add up to Nigeria becoming self-sufficient in rice production for the first time in 50 years, that will be a huge achievement. And the signs are that this is by no means impossible. Nigeria's food importation bill has already been reduced from N1.1 trillion in 2011 to N648 billion in 2012, and over 8 million metric tonnes of food were added to the domestic supply in 2012.

Chapter Five

THE CHALLENGE OF BLACK GOLD

One evening in June 1956 a group of British, German and Dutch engineers threw a party on their houseboat moored on the Niger Delta near the town of Oloibiri. Everyone in the local village was invited to see the discovery that was the cause of all the rejoicing. Some expected to hear that the foreigners had found a valuable new source of palm oil, the edible oil that had been exported from West Africa for hundreds of years. Instead they were shown a very different kind of oil. This was vicious black stuff, inedible but many times more valuable than the other sort. And it changed the course of Nigerian history. In the 60 years since that first exploratory well came up trumps, the government, as the majority shareholder in Nigeria's oil industry and a collector of tax and royalties on the crude produced by Western oil giants active in its territory, has banked an estimated US$1.6 trillion. And Nigeria has become Africa's largest oil producer, pumping more than two million barrels per day and with more than 36 billion barrels of proven reserves.

Not unnaturally, the people of the Delta at first saw oil as a gift from God. But by the 1980s the Nigerian economy had fallen victim to a strain of what economists call the

"Dutch Disease", a precipitous decline following a windfall boom based on the exploitation of a natural resource. Only this time it was brought on not by tulips but by oil.

Since independence in 1960, a string of corrupt military-led dictatorships squandered the nation's mineral wealth. If during those decades the country had been run by men of Aristotelian virtue, then Nigeria would now be the most prosperous country in Africa by some margin. Instead, billions were siphoned off each year by army strongmen and billions more by corrupt officials in the oil bureaucracy. Meanwhile, those on whose land the oil was discovered found their fishing grounds devastated by pollution, their crops ravaged by oil spills and gas flares and little in the way of development to show for producing the wealth of Nigeria.

This spawned a backlash as community tensions turned to anger and an organised militant expression through pipeline explosions and kidnappings of foreign oil workers in the Delta by local militia. A mixture of environmental, political and socio-economic grievances, sometimes with links to organized criminality, drove the violence. Environmentalists, human rights activists and fair trade advocates around the world have championed the cause of the local people and oil giants active in the area such as Exxon, Chevron, and Shell have found themselves the subject of widespread criticism.

A 2009 amnesty for militants featured large cash hand-outs and training programs helped restore calm, along with the fact that Jonathan is an ethnic Ijaw from Bayelsa state in the Delta. However the long-term peace is far from assured.

The country's top oil officials are technically and

commercially competent. But self-dealing, patronage and chronic politicization often blocks development and questionable bureaucratic meddling can delay contracting and project roll out for years at a time. Meanwhile billions in oil revenues set aside for national development do not reach beneficiaries, mostly due to endemic corruption and waste.

These are the problems that the Jonathan administration inherited. The rebellion in the Delta undermined security and development. High security costs and maturing onshore reservoirs left the country as an underachiever in relation to its full potential and decades of poor sector management have diverted funds away from Nigerian oil and gas development.

And yet, under the Jonathan administration, the industry has undergone a number of reforms. Perhaps the most remarkable restructuring that has taken place is that indigenous oil and natural gas companies have grown exponentially. And then there has been the emergence of a successful petro-chemical and fertilizer industry, converting natural gas into secondary products vital for the growth of the country's economy.

Since 2009, indigenous companies, in partnership with foreign technical and financial partners, have purchased assets worth almost $10 billion from the world's big energy groups. Shell, Total of France, Eni of Italy and Chevron and ConocoPhillips of the US have all sold large onshore, and some offshore, oilfields to Nigerian oil companies, such as Seplat, Oando and Shoreline Natural Resources. Wale Tinubu, chief executive of Lagos-based Oando says that home-grown oil companies are set to account for nearly a quarter of the country's oil production within five years, up from about 10 per cent today and 1-2 per cent five years ago. "The sector could be up to 600,000 barrels a day in five years," he argues.[1]

Shell is now close to sealing the deal for their divestment of several Nigerian oilfields, for about $5 billion, to domestic buyers. The price tag for the four oilfields and a key pipeline co-owned by Shell (30%), France's Total (10%) and Eni of Italy (5%) has doubled since initial estimates towards the end of 2013. The rise highlights the financial muscle of a cluster of Nigerian oil companies that have emerged as prominent players in the country's hydrocarbon industry. Nigerian oil traders-cum-producers Taleveras and Aiteo have offered $2.6bn for the largest oilfield, known as Oil Mining Licence 29. "It is a lot of money," said a banker involved in the process. "It is a great display of the strength of the Nigerian indigenous oil industry."

Foreign banks traditionally facilitated these types of oilfield deals – if possible at all – but Nigerian banks have tapped international capital markets to raise long-term dollar financing through bonds and syndicated loans and are using the proceeds to fund local oil companies.

Domestic oil and gas companies aggressive expansion as IOC's move offshore have resulted in assets worth $5bn changing hands, truly reshaping Nigeria's 60-year-old oil industry. In this continuous divestment spree which began in 2010, the IOCs are expected to divest over 20 oil blocks with not less than 4 billion barrels of oil equivalent per day and a monetary value of about $11.5 billion before the end of 2014.

So what explains the multinational oil corporations' sudden willingness to sell their onshore assets and concentrate instead on deepwater offshore operations? The Western media in particular has portrayed it as a flight from a region that has proved to be more trouble than it's worth. For a long time, of course, such an option was not viable because there was no market for the oil licenses they held and the hardware they had installed. But with the emergence of Nigerian companies with money to spend, suddenly the oil giants could make a dignified exit. Indeed, some commentators reckon some of the indigenous newcomers have actually overpaid. Seplat, for example, bought licenses from Shell that were due to expire in five or six years, and asked investors in London to back them on the promise that they would be able to negotiate decent renewal terms.

The industry is changing because it is increasingly possible for national actors to assume roles that they previously thought could only be taken by the established international oil companies. Firstly, the oil majors have not moved out of Nigeria. They have instead chosen to focus on developing the huge offshore fields. There could be up to a dozen fields offshore Nigeria that hold more than a million barrels a day and could be up for development once the legislative obstacles are removed.

But also, over time, the oil majors have changed from full-service operators who ran everything from test bores to pipelines into massive clearing-houses for contracts. Many aspects of the business, from seismic analysis to drilling itself have increasingly been farmed out to local operators. A natural next step for a number of such companies was to become upstream licence-holders in their own right.

"What you might lose in terms of international exposure, you gain in regional and local knowledge," said an oil industry consultant. "The idea is that you as a local player can manage these assets more effectively than would the big oil companies. Yes, you lose some economies of scale, but you gain a better working relationship with local communities, with labour unions, with the NNPC, the Government and local stakeholders in general, because you are simply closer to the problems. And that is the big change of the model that's been happening during the Jonathan era."

Seplat appears to be a good example of what might be called the "indigenous producer dividend". When it bought Shell's first blocks to be auctioned they were producing around 15,000 barrels/day, according to one senior Nigerian oil executive. Today they are running at 60,000 bpd, and heading towards 90,000. With oil averaging comfortably over $100/barrel, such a performance has not been lost on Western investors. In early 2014, Seplat raised $500 million through a listing on stock markets in both the UK and Nigeria. "Other Nigerian exploration and production oil companies will follow us," said ABC Orjiako, chairman of Seplat. "It will not surprise me if we see more IPOs."

Seplat's experience shows that while the delay in the passage of the Petroleum Industry Bill has condemned billions of dollars of vital investment to the side-lines, Nigeria's oil and gas industry – contrary to popular perception – has not come to a halt. One industry source argues that the 15

Nigerian companies that are currently active in the market is likely to double within five years and the existing operators will grow rapidly in the same period.

Take Shoreline International Nigeria. Run by Nigerian entrepreneur Kola Karim, it struck up a partnership with the Heritage Oil, a Jersey-based oil and gas exploration and production company founded by the British businessman Tony Buckingham, to buy underperforming oil fields from Shell, Total and Eni for $850 million in November 2012. Since then it has increased production while simultaneously reducing losses from oil theft. This has been achieved by engaging with local communities and involving them in the business, according to Karim. "It is a challenge that needs to be tackled by multiple stakeholders in a multifaceted way," he said.

Karim's business interests span construction, power generation and telecoms across sub-Saharan Africa, and extended to joint ventures with Costain, the UK support services group, and Schlumberger, the US-based oil services company. A patron of the Lagos Polo Club – who has played polo with the Duke of Cambridge and Prince Harry at Lord Lloyd-Webber's private estate – his aim is to build an indigenous group capable of becoming a significant upstream oil operator in Africa's biggest energy industry.

And Shoreline is not the only success story. In January 2013, the Toronto-quoted Oando – one of the most ambitious of the home-grown energy groups – acquired the Nigerian business of the US oil group ConocoPhillips for a total of $1.79 billion, taking on onshore and offshore interests producing 43,000 barrels of oil a day. On the subject of the problems confronted by oil companies in the Delta, Oando's Wale Tinubu says: "This is a local problem and you need local expertise." He adds that the key is to involve communities in protecting pipelines and that indigenous companies are more adept at working in the difficult conditions that prevail in the area.

The Nigerian companies, it is argued, understand what the community drivers are. Most communities want access to power, therefore the answer is for the companies operating in the region to share it. If that means installing a turbine that is too big for the company's needs and offering the excess capacity to the local people then so be it. "Today that should almost be standard operating procedure," says one insider. "The IOCs today must be much more strategic in their thinking, inclusive in their management, and work with other agencies to achieve the best results. Much more can be achieved by scaling up, literally connecting one road with another."

And once the local community has a stake in something, the signs are they will cherish rather than destroy it. During riots in early 2000, everything bearing a Mobil logo was burned to the ground, even a $3 million community centre. The school was saved because local mothers joined hands and physically surrounded the building.

But while Nigerians have more of a stake in the exploitation of the country's prime national resource than ever before, not everyone is happy. Many observers have voiced their concern that the Jonathan administration has concentrated too much power in the hands of the Petroleum

Minister, Diezani Alison-Madueke. "The older guard, the big IOCs [International Oil Companies], think Diezani has been a disaster, and they are very vocal in saying so," says one supporter. "But for the new generation she has been a strong promoter of 'local content'. Going against the old establishment and created a new and, for indigenous companies, more level, playing field.

"It is a complete transition within the industry, and it is a natural progression. It is not a nationalisation, but it is about Nigeria coming of age. We are seeing young and well-trained Nigerians able to take more control of its industry. If Alison-Madueke had not taken charge – with the backing of Jonathan – you would not have seen this emergence of local champions. She is controversial, but at the moment her reputation is very one-sided. Her legacy depends on what lens you are looking through. For young Nigerian companies, like Seplat, Oando and Shoreline, she has been an enabler, and this is the first time they are really seeing the opportunity to participate in the upstream industry."

Another enabler for local Nigerian companies to play more active roles in the industry is the Local Content Act – a forerunner to the Petroleum Industry Bill – which was signed by Jonathan on 22 April 2010.

The Act, which directly affects operating companies, contractors, sub-contractors and service providers, seeks to increase indigenous participation in the oil and gas industry by prescribing minimum thresholds for the use of local services and materials and to promote the employment of Nigerian staff in the industry.

The local content act requires that first consideration be given to Nigerian companies when contracts are awarded for oil blocks, licences and all other projects. Indeed, some of the most important aspects of the Act are to develop indigenous skills across the oil and gas value chain; promote indigenous ownership of assets and use of indigenous assets in oil and gas operations; enhance the multiplier effect to promote the establishment of support industries; and create customised training and sustainable employment opportunities.

But Alison-Madueke's supporters argue that foreign operators such as Shell are not involved in a flight from Nigeria but merely re-orientating their businesses. "They are now heading to the deeper water offshore plays in higher margin areas where they have a comparative advantage," says a senior oil executive. "To a large extent it is the new market norm in Nigeria: rationalising your asset portfolios. Five years ago you could not have done that, the IOCs were the dominant holders of acreage. But today you have Seplat, Oando, and Shoreline and many more coming. They are all terrific engineers, who know what they are doing. And they are utilising their comparative advantage: they are Nigerians. If you know how to handle the security, if you are at one with the communities, it is really a great investment worth a premium.

"Despite a lot of negative publicity Shell has provided excellent training in Nigeria. The amount of people that have passed through the Shell organisation and/or its scholarships, is truly incredible. And they are all Nigerians. With this in mind Shell has been mistreated. They were dealt a difficult position. Wrong decisions were at times certainly taken, and they should have been much more active with the communities from the start. But this idea that you are dealing with the devil is downright wrong."

One of Alison-Madueke's cardinal sins in the eyes of her detractors is her failure to get the Petroleum Industry Bill (PIB) through Parliament. A PIB of one sort or another has been in the works for 15 years. Its origins date back to President Obasanjo's first term in office, when in 2000 he set up a body called the Oil and Gas Reform Implementation Committee (OGIC), with a mandate to take a comprehensive look at Nigeria's oil and gas sector which was still governed by laws and regulations that had been around since the 1960s. The OGIC was led by Rilwanu Lukman, a veteran petroleum engineer who had two spells as Nigeria's Petroleum Resources Minister, from 1986 to 1990 and 2008 to 2010. Revived by Yar'Adua after it slipped in the list of priorities, the committee submitted its report in 2008, and its recommendations for a radical overhaul for Nigeria's energy sector were swiftly approved by the Federal Executive Council. This became the actual Petroleum Industry Bill presented to the National Assembly in 2009 – and there it has remained ever since, growing ever longer and more complex. Meanwhile, oil majors are holding back on many billions of dollars of investment as they wait to see what the provisions of the new law will mean for them.

It is a very Nigerian paradox. Everyone knows the oil and gas sector, the cornerstone of sub-Saharan Africa's second largest economy, has underperformed for a generation. But while there is much common ground among most stakeholders on the severity of the illness, there is no such consensus on the cure.

The latest version of the bill proposes changes that will improve transparency, unveiling previously cloaked royalty payments, as well as going public with the various company tax incentives. Indeed, the PIB is meant to change everything from fiscal terms to the structure of the NNPC, converting from a somewhat conflicted regulatory agency with vast equity stakes in the country's oil blocks to a national oil company run on commercial principles. But investors are concerned that the PIB, in its current form, will presage a more aggressive fiscal regime – especially for deep-water exploration.

The Petroleum Industry Bill was an issue that the Jonathan administration inherited. People have known for many years that the oil and gas sector in Nigeria hasn't worked for the state, though it has worked fairly well for some well-connected interests. There have been benefits for the few against the interests of the many. The report commissioned during the Yar'Adua administration stated that the NNPC wasn't fit for purpose. There needed to be a thorough overhaul, which led into the drafting of the PIB, and it was supposed to create a single homogenous framework for oil and gas in Nigeria.

It was actually quite a simple idea but, as is often the way in Nigeria, a simple idea in practice became very complex and detailed. It became more and more controversial, longer and longer. What started off with four basic principles that could have been summed up on a single a page, instead became a 400-page bill, which is what Jonathan and the oil minister inherited. It was a very Nigerian dilemma. Everyone knew the system was broken, but it was much harder to find consensus on how to fix it between the various stakeholders. Reform in Nigeria is as much a political process as a technical issue, particular in an area as sensitive as hydrocarbons. Vested interests from all sides were against the Bill from the very beginning, some because they thought it went too far, others because it did not go far enough. Lots of people used it as a platform to play politics. It has spent years in parliament, and is always very close to being passed.

The new bill has the ambitious task of bringing together 16 different existing laws and numerous other regulations into one statute. Once passed, it would become the master reference law that governs the Nigerian petroleum industry – from the upstream division (exploratory, development and production activities) through the midstream (gas processing) to downstream (servicing, refining, distribution, transportation, marketing/retailing). Given the breadth of its ambition, perhaps it is not surprising that the incarnation of the bill that was being worked on in mid-2014 was the nineteenth version of it. Some experts suggest it should have been broken up into three more manageable pieces of legislation devoted to fiscal reform, the downstream sector and the restructuring of the Nigerian National Petroleum Corporation (NNPC). "Everyone has a dog in this fight, so in terms of voting it is too problematic," says one senior oil executive.

The NNPC, in particular, has long been a headache. An overstaffed bureaucracy with opaque accounting standards, it has a workforce protected by powerful unions and a management tier made up of people all too often appointed on the basis of political considerations rather than competence. The NNPC has majority shares in all its Joint Ventures with the IOCs but repeatedly fails to make its share of payments towards ongoing projects, with the result that a number are dormant. Its four refineries also suffer from chronic underfunding which partly explains why Nigeria is so dependent upon petroleum product imports.

The resulting gridlock eroded the Nigerian petroleum sector's technical and commercial fundamentals. Oil reserves grew by less than 30 per cent over the 2000s—the lowest rate of all major African producers apart from Congo-Brazzaville. The last major discovery in the deep-water is more than a decade old, with over 20 awarded blocks sitting idle. Even without supply disruptions from theft and sabotage, and factoring in gains from the amnesty program, production in 2014 is barely at 2005 levels. Government data show output from aging onshore wells falling 10 to 12 per cent a year with scarce replacements. According to Wood Mackenzie, without serious investment production could fall 20 per cent by 2020. Meanwhile, exploitation of Nigeria's gas reserves—one of the largest in the world— was slowed by low political attention, underinvestment, infrastructure deficits, and power sector dysfunction.

Over time, such problems have reduced government's earnings from oil. Nigeria's aging reservoirs now require billions of dollars in extra operating costs each year to maintain even current production levels. The IOCs carry government's share of costs on roughly a quarter of all crude production, attracting average finance charges of nine per cent. Greater reliance on development offshore, which is governed by out-dated production sharing contracts that favour operators, reduces per barrel profits to the nation. Lost or trapped investment could top $50 billion, with the costs of deferred production higher still.

The PIB was designed to resolve the NNPC's perennial financing difficulties, to tackle the pervasive culture of corruption, and to create incentives for investment in gas production and processing – both for export and domestic consumption. But fierce lobbying over the bill between rival vested interests has produced a stalemate.

The Nigerian Finance Minister, Ngozi Okonjo-Iweala, addressed the topic of vested interests hijacking the PIB process in the Financial Times. "This draft law contains provisions to transform the oil and gas sector, including turning the NNPC into a commercial enterprise," she wrote. "This would open up the corporation and the oil industry, making them more transparent and accountable to Nigerians. Yet passage of the bill has been delayed in the National Assembly as a result of intensive lobbying by interest groups – some Nigerian, some foreign – who benefit from the status quo either through favourable oil deals or favourable treatment by the Nigerian tax system. We call on these groups to allow the bill's passage."

We can assume that the "foreign" lobbying referred to by Okonjo-Iweala is a reference to IOCs. One of the major

Kidnapped: Some of the 267 girls abducted by Islamist militants Boko Haram from a school in Chibok, northern Nigeria, in April 2014. This photograph, part of a 27 minute video distributed by Boko Haram to a French news agency, shows a teenage girl speaking under duress. (Youtube)

Bragging on Youtube: A video message from the alleged leader of the Islamist militant group Boko Haram, Abubakar Shekau, in which he claims responsibility for the abduction of the schoolgirls. Speaking in a mixture of Hausa and English, he threatens to 'sell them on the market' and declares war on Christians. (Youtube)

A young Jonathan: This picture was taken in 1974 at Mater Dei High School in Imiringi, Bayelsa State, when Jonathan was a 17 year-old student. (Champion Newspaper)

Meet The Jonathans: Pictures of the Nigerian First Family are rare. In a ThisDay exclusive in 2011 President Jonathan poses with his wife Patience and their son Ariweri (right) and daughter Aruabai (left). (ThisDay Style Magazine)

The President: Goodluck Jonathan, at the World Economic Forum meeting in Abuja in April 2014. (Sunday Alamba/AP)

A marriage of convenience: Jonathan as Deputy Governor of Bayelsa State greets his boss Diepreye Alamieyeseigha (right) at Port Harcourt International airport in 2004. Alamieyeseigha was subsequently convicted of corruption and jailed, opening the way for Jonathan to become Governor. (Nigerian National Library)

The President and the power behind the throne: Former President Umaru Yar 'Adua, who died in office in 2011, and his wife Hajiya Turai Yar 'Adua. She was accused of trying to hijack power while her husband was on his sick bed. (AFP/Getty Images)

The Kingmaker: Former President Olusegun Obasanjo played a critical role in the selection of Jonathan as Vice President. Seen here during a guard of honour inspection at Arlington County, Virginia, May 2001. (The Independent)

The Iron Lady: As Nigeria's first female Finance Minister, Ngozi Okonjo-Iweala is known for her tough stance against corruption. She is a former Managing Director at the World Bank. (ThisDay Live)

Phones for the millions: In 2013 one million women farmers were given mobile phones to make it easier to obtain the best prices for their produce. (National Library)

Billionaire: Businessman and philanthropist, Alhaji Aliko Dangote, the wealthiest black man in the world. (Business World Newspaper)

Burning Energy: Gas being flared near Port Harcourt in Rivers State in the Niger Delta. Flaring has caused tremendous damage to the environment and human health. (Nigerian Oil and Gas Weekly)

The new Business Elite: Kola Karim, CEO of Shoreline Energy International Plc, playing polo with Prince William and Prince Harry at the Kent & Curwen Royal Polo Cup in 2013. (Ernest Ekpenyong)

Turning Gas into Plastics: The Eleme Petrochemicals Company, owned by India's Indorama Corporation, was almost moribund before it was privatised, but will soon be Africa's largest petrochemicals plant. (Nigerian National Library)

The Emir: Lamido Sanusi, whose departure as head of the Nigerian Central Bank was accompanied by accusations of missing billions from the country's oil revenues and corruption at the bank. He was later crowned 'Emir of Kano,' one of the most significant religious positions in Nigeria. (Nigerian National Library)

Nigerian Godfather: James Ibori, former Governor of Delta state, was convicted and sentenced to 13 years in jail by Southwark Crown Court for money laundering and fraud. (Champion Newspaper)

Flying High: Stella Oduah-Ogiemwonyi, former Aviation Minister, who was dismissed in 12 February 2014 following corruption scandals. (The Sun Newspaper)

Man with a plan: As National Security Adviser, General Sambo Dasuki, championed a new strategy to defeat Boko Haram that did not rely solely on a military solution. (Champion Newspaper)

Fighting For Peace: Nigerian troops on another international mission in Mali in January 2013. Nigeria dispatched 1,200 men, the biggest deployment of any African nation, to assist in driving Islamist extremists from power in northern Mali. (Nigerian National Library)

Man with a plan: As National Security Adviser, General Sambo Dasuki, championed a new strategy to defeat Boko Haram that did not rely solely on a military solution. (National Library*)*

Devastation: Wreckage at a market place in Jos after two car bombs exploded at a bus terminal, on May 20, 2014, killing more than 100 people. (AFP/Getty Images)

disagreements between the government and the oil majors has been the new fiscal terms for the deepwater offshore wells. The government has based its calculations on worldwide industry costs whereas the IOCs take into account the higher cost of doing business in Nigeria due to their additional outlays on security. This is why many of the IOCs claim that the new PIB taxes will be among the highest in the world. This has led them hold off on investments until they such time as they know what kind of fiscal environment they will be dealing with.

"All the major offshore deep-water projects, all about $10 billion each, are just waiting for the PIB to happen," says one industry figure. "Gas fiscals are also a challenge. The government wanted to eliminate the AGFA (Associated Gas Framework Agreement) subsidy and make gas project economics standalone from oil. The ability to offset new gas investment against oil revenue is necessary to encourage domestic gas projects and some accommodation between government and industry needs to be reached to grow the gas market. But the PIB will likely pass next year, once re-election is not an issue any more. Then I think Jonathan will just push the bill through."

Under the new law, the NNPC would be stripped of much of its regulatory powers, unbundled and split into three successor companies that will be run as proper businesses. The first, known as the National Asset Management Corporation, will house the government's share of the joint venture operations with the big oil companies. The second, a new national oil company, will operate along commercial lines, as happens in other emerging market economies, and will take over the 130,000 barrels/day operations of the Nigeria Petroleum Development Company. Thirty percent of the shares in this new entity will be sold to the public via the Nigerian stock exchange. The third will be a national gas company. At least that's the plan.

Have they solved it? No they have not completely, but a few other parameters in the industry are starting to shift. The original idea of the PIB was to reshape the joint ventures, which have been the centre of the industry for the last 50 years, and ensure that they were going to work. But now even without the PIB, Shell has indicated that it wants to relinquish some of the assets that it holds. Indeed, as we have seen, Shell and others have disposed of some already.

For all the infighting and complexities, the Nigerian oil and gas sector is still a sector that is easy to get excited about. Nigeria's gas exploration drive has been suspended, but domestic gas and gas-fired power generation are likely be the main driver of the country's economic success in the coming years.

There has never been a robust inward market for the vast quantities of gas Nigeria possesses, and the opportunities are still very much emerging. The only real market for gas, until now, has been tied to a specific project, or for export as either liquefied natural gas from Bonny or the West African Gas Pipeline. But there is a real potential in Nigerian gas: despite its status as one of the world's major oil exporters, Ministry of Petroleum Resources officials are fond of describing Nigeria as a gas province with some oil, so huge are the reserves.

Nigeria LNG (NLNG) is a joint venture between NNPC, Shell, which is also the technical adviser, Total and Eni. NLNG has invested more than $15 billion in its Bonny Island plant – Africa's biggest – which can produce up to 21.8 million metric tons of the chilled gas a year, or almost 8 per cent of the world's total supply. It is already profitable, so profitable in fact that two more similar projects had been drawn up: Brass LNG and OK LNG, each with different sponsors and different political backers. However, project delays, cost increases associated with the construction of the LNG plants themselves and a collapse in LNG spot market rates combined to lead sponsors to pull out of the OK LNG plant and uncertainty over the timing of the Final Investment Decision (FID) on Brass. While gas is available for export, the scale of the investment involved in the LNG market means investors are reluctant to commit in the face of uncertainty.

Nigeria also has a number of promising gas to power and gas to industry projects, and has succeeded in building a growing and successful petrochemical and fertilizer industry. Notore Chemical Industries, which took over the failing Nigerian fertilizer parastatal NAFCOM in 2005, sells fertilizer directly to tens of thousands of farmers, most of them in the north of the country. It is one of the most startling examples of a successful privatization in Nigeria.

Indorama's Eleme plant, also in the Port Harcourt area, is about to become the largest petrochemical company in Africa. It produces feedstock for plastics both for export and for secondary industries within Nigeria, and has been at the center of a plastics product manufacturing boom in Rivers state. The Dangote group recently raised a $9-billion facility (largely from Nigerian banks) to support the construction of Sub-Saharan Africa's largest refinery as well as a petrochemical and fertilizer plant.

Nigeria remains a vibrant market. In the past, five dominant IOCs drove all before them. Now they have been joined by the new wave of dynamic indigenous companies, which are all hungry for more. There is a buoyant investment market and compared to other territories, such as the deep-water sector in Ghana, Nigeria is still one of the cheapest countries to enter. But above all there is documentary evidence of huge oil and gas reserves within its borders. Unlike when the foreign engineers held their party on a houseboat near Oloibiri that day in 1956 there is no mystery about what lies underground.

Chapter Six

CONFRONTING THE
WEB OF CORRUPTION

It was a bright hot day at lunch-time on 9 December 2012, and Dr Kamene Okonjo, the 85-year-old mother of the Nigerian Finance Minister, was serving drinks to workers outside her house in the small town of Ogwashi-Uku, in the heart of the Delta. Suddenly, she heard an unexpected noise and a gang of men approached her. Before anyone could do anything she was immediately grabbed by the men, bundled into a car and driven away.

Kidnappings are not uncommon in the oil-producing region of Nigeria, with foreign oil businessmen being the usual targets. In recent years, however, relatives of rich Nigerian businessmen, politicians and international footballers have become increasingly vulnerable. The kidnap menace has also spread to Lagos, Nigeria's largest city and its economic hub. Victims of "express kidnappings", as they are dubbed, are rarely kept for more than a fortnight and most are freed, after a cash ransom has been handed over, within three or four days.

But the abduction of Dr Okonjo was no ordinary kidnapping. In this case there were no demands for money or favours. And yet, after five days, the academic was dropped off, unharmed, on a main road near her home. All the signs are that it was a warning aimed at her daughter, Dr Ngozi Okonjo-Iweala, the Finance Minister. Okonjo-Iweala had received threats relating to her attempts to stop oil subsidies being misappropriated and it is more than likely that her elderly mother was targeted because she had been an outspoken opponent of the corruption, which has long prevented the country from fulfilling its potential.

"Corruption is a very big problem in Nigeria," said Dr Okonjo-Iweala. "I am not walking around feeling afraid. I really am not. But that doesn't mean that I am stupid and not careful. Because when you get threats you cannot ignore them. Even as late as last week I got another one. Now the President has been kind enough to double my security. But when you are doing these things, fighting against terrorism and corruption you cannot give up. We cannot give our country over to these people."

The kidnapping of the mother of Nigeria's combative Finance Minister was shocking on its own terms but it also put a wider malaise under the spotlight. Corruption has been endemic and systematic in Nigeria since it came into existence as an independent state. Richard Dowden, director of the Royal African Society, wrote in 2008: "Corruption pervades Nigerian life so broadly and deeply that it is hard to imagine life in Nigeria if it were suddenly to end. Without a little something a policeman will not investigate a crime, a journalist will not write up a politician's speech, a politician will not speak to a constituent, a tax inspector will not sign off your tax return... In Nigeria every contact between an official and an individual seems to involve an extra payment... To check your name on the voter's register, to get a passport, to pass through a roadblock – all involve a few notes changing hands. It may be 20 naira for a policeman or it may be $20 million that an international company pays a minister for an oil concession or a road-building contract. Everybody pays."

Nowhere is this culture of graft more damaging than when it comes to Nigeria's great natural bounty: oil. An estimated $400 billion of the country's oil revenue has been stolen or misspent since independence in 1963, according to Nuhu Ribadu, who ran Nigeria's principal anti-corruption agency, the Economic and Financial Crimes Commission, as its founding chairman from 2004 to 2007. And despite efforts to eradicate it over the years, the theft of public money remains a problem of crisis proportions. In 2012 a leaked Petroleum Revenue Special Task Force report into Nigeria's oil and gas industry revealed that mismanagement and corruption in that sector was still costing the country billions of dollars each year, with the problem persisting throughout the system, from the awarding of contracts to the sale of refined products.

The state-owned Nigerian National Petroleum Corporation (NNPC), described as "one of the world's most closed oil companies" by The Economist, was condemned by NGOs, notably Global Witness, for having the worst record of 44 national and foreign companies they examined. Various attempts have been made to dilute the power of the NNPC and International Oil Companies (IOCs) but none of them has met with much success. In the early 1990s, the plan was to transfer some of their assets to an independent, indigenous private sector with genuine ambition and capacity. But this process was marred by a corrupt form of political patronage, with hosts of hangers-on securing licences that they turned over for substantial personal profit. Even the return to civilian rule and an apparent move towards competitive tendering could not break the spiral of corruption and the widely held perception that political factors play a disproportionately important part in the management of the sector.

When a letter written by Lamido Sanusi, the bespectacled, bow-tied Central Bank Governor, calling for an investigation into billions of dollars of unreconciled funds was leaked in 2012 it fuelled the perception of an untouchable industry operating above the law. What happened next, though, was even more revealing. Government officials questioned Sanusi's motives, pointing out that there was plenty of evidence that all was not well with the finances of the Bank itself. They argued that his intervention was opportunistic, more of a diversionary tactic than an example of principled whistle-blowing. This view was fuelled by the Governor's apparent uncertainty over the figures involved, which over a few weeks ranged from $10 billion to close to $50 billion.

As claim and counter claim swirled around the media, the Financial Reporting Council of Nigeria (FRCN) was commissioned to investigate the operations of the Central Bank of Nigeria (CBN) under Sanusi. Its report, released on

June 7, 2013, stated in part: "It is important that quick and decisive action is taken so that opposition to the Federal Government does not take advantage of the information and use it to attack the government that Your Excellency was aware of the lax in the CBN and allowed it to stay for (partisan) political reasons….It is also important that the CBN governor and/or deputy governors do not decide earlier than Your Excellency as they may resign their appointments to foreclose the action of the Federal Government and any action taken thereafter shall be taken as politically motivated."

The damning report made far-reaching allegations of financial impropriety and outrageous spending against the Central Bank Governor. Some of the allegations related to Sanusi personally, whilst others highlighted the abuse of due process that characterised his administration of the bank. It was claimed that Sanusi:

- Spent N1.257 billion on "lunch for policemen and private guards" in 2012 alone

- Made bogus payments to airlines for currency distribution across Nigeria

- Approved billions of naira in ambiguous payments to invoices referred to as "Contribution to Internal National Security" and the "Centre of Excellence" – fuelling speculation that they were routed to states controlled by the opposition All Progressives Congress (APC)

• Paid N38.233 billion to the "Nigerian Security
Printing and Minting Company Plc" in 2011, for the
printing of bank notes, whereas the turnover of the
entire printing and minting company in 2011 was
recorded as N29.370 billion – far less than what the
company reportedly earned from the CBN alone

• Was closely connected to a bank account, with a
balance of N1.423 billion, that Sanusi had held for
an unidentified customer since 2008.

Sanusi strongly denied the claims and described the allegations
of financial recklessness as a malicious and calculated attempt
to mislead President Jonathan. However, based on the
Council's recommendations, Jonathan suspended Sanusi on
21 February 2014, pending investigations into the alleged
improprieties that had occurred during his tenure. He justified
his delay in acting against the Governor by saying he had
proceeded with caution for fear of destabilising Nigeria's fragile
banking system, which had scarcely recovered from the near
fatal collapse of 2008. But as the suspension came after Sanusi
had repeated his allegations to a National Assembly
committee, the Governor's supporters said he was being
punished for embarrassing people in power.

The President responded by pointing out that
documentary evidence showed that the Government had
already begun a review of reports of illicit dealings
surrounding Sanusi's governorship at the Central Bank in late
2012 – several months prior to his allegations. Sanusi was

then questioned by President Jonathan in mid 2013. It added that Sanusi had been suspended rather than dismissed, and maintained he had a case to answer. Any prospect of charges being brought against the suspended Governor evaporated four months after his removal, however, when he was selected to succeed his late great uncle as Emir of Kano, an appointment that had the convenient effect of giving him immunity from prosecution.

The move against Sanusi showed that the Jonathan administration was not prepared to turn a blind eye to the oil revenues missing from state accounts, and the corrupt governance of an industry that was central to Nigeria's economic wellbeing. Indeed Jonathan instructed his Finance Minister Ngozi Okonjo-Iweala to get to the root of the problem. Few people in Nigerian public life has a record as distinguished as that of Okonjo-Iweala. As a former number two at the World Bank, she came to office with a glittering reputation and she was determined to mount a proper investigation of the NNPC's finances. And that meant operating forensically, examining its paperwork department by department, laboriously reconciling every invoice. No one was more aware than she was of how weary the Nigerian people had become of hearing different figures being bandied about from one day to the next.

"It is no good going out and quoting a figure when you are not sure of what you are doing," she said. "You can't go out one day and quote $50 billion and the next day you say it's 20 and the third day you say it's 12 and the fourth day you say it's 10. The people become sceptical. But more important than that is to try and get this money back to the Treasury. After saying all those figures who is working to get those money back and setting up a system to make sure this doesn't happen? It is not very sexy to build systems and institutions. It takes time and nobody wants to discuss it. If we don't build them in this country nobody will, and that's why I am here. It is not enough to sit out there and have a wonderful reputation when nobody is fighting. We have to come in here and fight. That's what we are doing. Someone has to do the work".[1]

The real amount of the missing oil money emerged during a meeting between Sanusi, the Petroleum Minister, the Head of the NNPC and the Finance Minister. In fact, NNPC was required to remit $10.8 billion to the Treasury – a vast amount but far less than reported. "Sanusi confirmed the number himself," said a ministerial aide present at the meeting. "There was never $50 billion missing. He just wanted to make headlines to cover up his own tracks. But everyone bought into it and the international media printed every word. There was no fact-checking before they went to press."

Okonjo-Iweala felt that this finding merited the commissioning of an even more thorough probe and in May 2014 – in the face of stiff resistance from vested interests and their proxies in the system – she announced that top international accountancy firm PWC was to conduct a forensic audit of NNPC's books. Its report promises to bring some transparency to an industry that under earlier governments was marked by back-room deals and double-dealing, sometimes involving businesses that rank among the world's biggest companies.

Leaked diplomatic cables, published by Wikileaks, showed just how much access the Anglo-Dutch oil giant Shell had to the machinery of government. After the US ambassador Robin Renee Sanders met Ann Pickard, then Shell's vice-president for sub-Saharan Africa, in her embassy in Abuja on 20 October 2009, she later reported: "She said the GON [government of Nigeria] had forgotten that Shell had seconded people to all the relevant ministries and that Shell consequently had access to everything that was being done in those ministries." The cable concludes with the observation that the oil executive had tended to be guarded in discussion with US officials: "Pickard has repeatedly told us she does not like to talk to USG [US government] officials because the USG is 'leaky'. She may be concerned that... bad news about Shell's Nigerian operations will leak out."

Shell is the most established of the IOCs operating in Nigeria, and close to the centre of several scandals of its own. As the lead player in Nigeria Liquefied Natural Gas, it helped award construction contracts in the late 1990s and early 2000s that generated controversy and scandal when a subsidiary of US services giant Halliburton, a lead member of the winning consortium, admitted that it had paid huge bribes to government officials to win the contracts.

Shell was also to feature in the controversy over OPL245, one of a series of oil blocks awarded on a discretionary basis under military rule in the 1990s. OPL245 stood out because it was a particularly attractive block and because the oil minister at the time of the award, Chief Dan Etete, had effectively awarded it to his own company, Malabu Oil and Gas. Industry insiders later maintained that Etete, like other beneficiaries at the time, was holding shares for the then military ruler, Sani Abacha. What is certainly true is that Abacha's death in 1998 and the return to civilian rule a year later led to an unseemly scramble for OPL245. At various stages, interests close to the then President, Olusegun Obasanjo, and his estranged deputy, Atiku Abubakar, claimed to be close to a deal to deliver the block to Shell, which had seen the data and was keen to step into the acreage in the same way that other companies had bought into licences awarded to other friends and associates of senior military officers in the 1990s.

When the Jonathan administration took power in 2010, it inherited a situation – due to decades of political manoeuvring and disputes – over competing consultancy contracts, with no prospect that development of the oil block and the production of taxable revenue, might ever commence. The solution was not elegant: the government bought the field back from Malabu, and then sold it to Shell and ENI of Italy, prompting outrage from Global Witness and other anti-corruption campaigners over the fact that two international companies and the Nigerian government had colluded to make the former oil minister a billionaire.

Shell and ENI denied any wrongdoing and a Presidency source noted there had been no similar expressions of concern when other IOCs had completed on similar deals with assorted associates of the former military regime, in several instances at even more inflated costs. "Government is about making the best of options that sometimes are not ideal," he said. "With 245 we inherited a problem, which we could have left in litigation that might have lasted years. This was the best way to get the acreage into production. And any benefit to Malabu would be dwarfed by what others received from the same licensing round."

While the OPL245 case involved a real-life asset, in a society accustomed to impropriety in high places – one former Governor, James Ibori, ended up in jail in the UK in 2012 and another, Diepre Alamieyeseigha, received a presidential pardon a few months later – political factors are as likely to initiate a whispering campaign as any particular scandal or body of evidence.

The President himself has personal experience of just such chicanery. In an interview with the authors, he said: "When I was the Governor of Bayelsa state [2005 to 2007] there was one evening when I was arriving in Abuja, and the first thing I saw on the seven o'clock news was that 'Governor Jonathan has stolen $50 billion in corruption'. $50 billion! I had just been made Governor at that time. Do they even know the budget and income for all of Bayelsa state? How could I have stolen $50 billion? It is not physically possible. But that did not matter to those who made the allegation. No, it was ridiculous, but no one was checking the facts. It made the headlines, the national news, and still no one had even questioned the source? Not one!"

Nor has his wife been immune from such attacks. Allegations of impropriety against Patience Jonathan also date back to the days when her husband was Bayelsa State Governor. While there appears little doubt that she was investigated by the EFCC, its chairman at the time, Nuhu Ribadu, who stood against Jonathan for the Presidency in 2011, insisted there was no case to answer: "The way we worked at the EFCC was that if there was a petition against you, we looked to see if there's substance in it, if we can verify and see whether it was something that was worth looking into. A lot of the petitions were politically motivated. Some of them we were ready to go to court, some of them we were investigating, some of them were not worth investigating... When I declared my intention to contest elections, somebody from the media asked me about the Jonathan case. I said, 'No, I have never taken statement from this woman [his wife]. I have never taken her in for anything.' I don't even understand the controversy and I'm shocked about it. I will be the last person to be used to malign people simply because it is convenient. I would not do it."[2]

Similarly, allegations made against the Minister of Petroleum Resources Diezani Alison-Madueke have come to nothing despite no fewer than 200 summonses from the National Assembly – a body notorious for its reputation for shaking down officials or businessmen under pressure. "The investigations [into the affairs of Alison-Madueke] have just commenced," says one government insider. "Jonathan will see this through. He will take the decision when he has the full picture. He is not jumping into actions. He does not want every Minister to constantly worry that someone is going to whisper something bad into the ear of the President. No, he wants them to focus on their job, and do it well. If they have done something wrong the system will provide the evidence and they will be dismissed and their crimes will be handled by a judge."

This cautious, relatively moderate approach has its detractors but the Jonathan camp insist that the President is on the right track. Instead of just sacking the officials implicated in the various scandals and sending them to jail – the modus operandi of the Obasanjo regime – Jonathan seeks to reform the system from within by removing the easy opportunities for corruption. His policy is to de-regulate and reconstruct the parastatals, or what he calls the "centres of corruption". But this policy is difficult to implement given the power and influence of the vested interests that have dominated Nigeria's political and business scene for so long. When Nuhu Ribadu was at the EFCC, the President's party had strong majorities in both the Senate and the House of Representatives, and control of 30 of Nigeria's 36 State Governors. The international community fully supported the new anti-corruption initiative. But it foundered after the change of government in 2007, amid accusations that the campaign had been more about eliminating political opponents than good governance. Ribadu is having none of it. "When you fight corruption," he drily noted, "corruption fights back."

The President's aides are nevertheless optimistic. "Jonathan wanted to build institutions that were reliant on systems and checks instead of strong men," said one political aide. "He wants the institutions to be strong, not the people who govern them."

Together with the Finance Minister Jonathan has gradually been building up these systems. They include the Integrated Personnel & Payroll Information System whereby every government worker is paid electronically rather than manually which was previously the case; the Integrated Tax Administration System which allows citizens to file their tax returns and pay their taxes online: and the Treasury Single Account - that enables the Minister of Finance to access an overview of all the money in the system. "These are the systems that fight corruption. They are not very sexy, but they are efficient," said Constance Ikokwu, media adviser to the Finance Minister. "With the help of these electronic platforms we have saved millions of dollars. Nigeria doesn't need powerful individuals, it needs solid systems like these."

"You need to understand how Jonathan deals with things. He gives every situation the time it needs – enough time to see the evidence. He will always do what he thinks needs to be done, based on the information that is available to him, and he has more information than us."

This new-found reliance on due process when dealing with corruption was illustrated by the N255 million BMW scandal involving the former Minister of Aviation, Stella Oduah. She was a long-time associate of Jonathan, who worked closely with him during the 2011 campaign, but the President refused to interfere with the investigation into her actions and when its findings were delivered, he fired her face-to-face. "Stella did more for the Nigerian aviation sector in two years, than any of her predecessors had done altogether," said one political aide. "The BMW affair was irresponsible. But many Ministers have these bulletproof cars. Ask the Governor of Lagos what he paid for his fleet of cars! I think it was sad to see Stella go, but Jonathan has no tolerance for corruption so he allowed the system to work.

According to one well-connected international consultant: "If there ever was a President in Nigeria who could understand and tackle these issues it would be someone with a background in environmental issues from the Delta, just like Jonathan. Someone who knows what that kind of corruption does for the communities, how it literally destroys them. Yar'Adua's father was a Minister in the First Republic, Obasanjo was a long-serving General. Jonathan, however, ten years before he was President was really nobody at all, and would have been much closer to ordinary people's perception of how tough life could be.

"I do remember once, it was the QaedaEarth Summit in Rio in 2012 on Sustainable Development. It got kind of downgraded in the end, I think. Obama and lots of other top people weren't going, but Jonathan still insisted on going. I started thinking – is this some back-channel to talk to the Chinese or something, and why is he so persistent? And so I talked to not one of his allies, but in fact someone in government that had actually fallen out with Jonathan, and even he said that 'No Jonathan genuinely believes, and is interested in these environmental issues and wants to be part of that debate.'"

Jonathan's supporters argue that his record shows that the President can be ruthless. Apart from his removal of Oduah – who many had considered untouchable – they note he sacked

General Azazi, his National Security Adviser, to whom he was very close, his Chief of Staff, Mike Oghiadomhe, and the Chairman of the Party, Bamanga Tukur. He also dismissed the Power Minister, Barth Nnaji, following his alleged involvement in two companies that benefited from the ongoing privatisation in the power sector. Even the Army Chief and the head of the police have been replaced. "He does make decisions now and again that really surprise people," says one observer. "You cannot survive in Nigeria without having a ruthless streak."

And Jonathan has a formidable supporter in his Finance Minister Okonjo-Iweala. "I don't want to sound like a one-woman anti-corruption squad," she says. "No one can do this alone. But at least I can visibly fight and score some successes. The President has never stopped me. Contrary to what people may think he takes the problem of corruption very seriously and he has never stopped me fighting these people.

"But you need to be fighting sensibly, you cannot fight everything. I cannot even tell you those things that I have stopped. I have stopped many things that would have cost this government money. But it is not something you run out in the street and start talking about. But those who are involved in it they know. And sometimes doing this is dangerous, but it has to be done and who else will do it? Is it those same people who say Nigeria is a corrupt country that will come here to fight it? The answer is no! The Nigerians themselves have to do it. Just don't sit there and complain. If we all did something small, we would not just have this moaning and groaning about it. If someone offers you a bribe, don't take it!

If you see someone do it and you can do something to make them stop, which I have done, then do it."

The President agreed: "The various corruptions commissions, like the EFCC, were more like warring dogs – they were fighting, barking and biting all the time. Before you knew it someone would have written a letter to them saying someone had stolen money from them and then they would prosecute this man or woman and place hand-cuffs on and show it all on television. It was a big spectacle for everyone to see it.

"And so I think during this time people did not even have the time or chance to defend themselves. They were always watching their backs, not knowing if anyone would report them to the EFCC. It became a political weapon that was used against your enemy. It was like terror, people became so intimidated.

"But did that intimidation solve corruption? If the terror was the answer, then there should be less corruption today? We had so many years of this. But we have corruption, and it got worse during this time, so we can see that this kind of political intimidation does not solve the problem".

Jonathan's approach is informed, at least in part, by his experience of the armed robbery issue. When it became more and more common after the civil war, largely due to the increase in the number of small arms in circulation, the military regime made it a capital offence. And in order to drive home the deterrence aspect, those found guilty were executed by firing squad – in public. Jonathan notes that this policy failed to wipe out armed robbery, however.

"So how do you stop corruption?" he asks. "Do you stop corruption by celebrating it on television? Showing it off to the world? Many had their hands tied and were prosecuted publicly, has that solved corruption? No, that does not solve the problem. We have seen that now. Just because previous Presidents did it that way, and barked very loudly, why should I do the same when we can see that it does not solve the problem? Then that is a waste of energy.

"I see that there are two approaches to how you can solve corruption in Nigeria today. First you must strengthen institutions that are strong enough to continue even if people cannot. This takes time, but this is what we must do. You do not solve this in one day. It is a big problem. We need big solution.

"Secondly, make sure that in those areas of massive corruption, you block it so you do not leave money lying around in a way so that somebody can easily take it. Take the area of fertiliser procurement, where we used to have massive corruption. Federal government used to spend up to $1 billion dollars every year to subsidize fertilizer for farmers, but so little of the product reached the actual farmers in the end.

"What eventually reached the farmers was half a bag of fertilizer and the other half of just grass or sand. Fertilizers were even recycled. But we have now cleared that up. Nobody is even talking about it anymore. Now there is no money that you can steal because now we have changed the systems and now the fertilizers are going directly to the farmers. There are no longer any middlemen. I think that is a big success."

Jonathan plans to extend this approach to the petroleum

sector. This is a another market where vast sums are spent on subsidies and much of the cash ends up in the hands of middlemen who smuggle subsidised products out of the country to sell at market prices elsewhere. "Why should we then continue with something that makes the richer men richer but does not help the ordinary people?" says Jonathan. "That is not what a Government should do. I wanted to stop that. It was not right. My approach to corruption is to strengthen institutions. That will take time, but it is the only way that I think will last. People will not last, but strong institutions can survive. I think it is the only way to eliminate corruption. But it will take time, it took time to build them in the West did it not? But now they are strong. You should give us that same time to build ours."

That is not to say that the President is prepared to let wrongdoer escape without punishment: "If people have committed a crime they should be arrested and prosecuted. But while that is going on we do not want to celebrate corruption, we do not want to broadcast it as entertainment. We do not build fear into our society. No, we build strong institutions that will prevent many from committing a crime in the first place."

Jonathan takes the view that human beings are "born greedy" and it is only by creating a system in which people realise that there will be consequences to their criminal behaviour that corruption can be curbed. The President's main reform in this area has been the implementation of the long delayed Freedom of Information Act. On May 24 2011, after 12 years in the making, the bill was finally completed and Jonathan signed it into statute.[3] Inspired by the US

Freedom of Information Act, the creation of such a piece of legislation had been the goal of Nigerian civil groups for more than a decade. The law guarantees public access to information held by public institutions and provides protection for whistle blowers. It had been vetoed by previous Presidents – Obasanjo claimed that it would compromise national security – but Jonathan pushed through the legislation within a year of assuming office.

The passage of the new law had media figures queuing up to pay tribute. The editor-in-Chief of Vanguard Newspapers Gbenga Adefaye wrote: "President Jonathan has really started well with this sign-post for good governance. By signing the FoI bill into law, the President has, more than anyone else, empowered the citizens to participate in the governance of their own affairs. The people can now legitimately seek public information, corroborate their facts and make useful suggestions towards achieving greater good for the majority. With access to information, citizens can fight corruption and closet government and confront the few who misappropriate our resources to themselves alone."

The former President of the Nigerian Union of Journalists, Adam Adeyemi, was no less fulsome: "I join other well-meaning Nigerians to commend Mr President for signing the bill into law. It will ensure good governance and help in the protection of human rights. It will expose corruption and other negative vices that hinder our socio-economic development in our society. Last week's passage of the Freedom of Information (FoI) Bill after 11 years of wanton hibernation in the National Assembly is a long walk to freedom."

And three pressure groups – The Right to Know initiative, Media Rights Agenda, and the Open Society Foundations – said in a joint statement: "The signing by Nigeria's President Goodluck Jonathan of a freedom of information (FOI) law is a victory for democracy, transparency, justice and development. With the new law, Nigerians finally have vital tools to uncover facts, fight corruption and hold officials and institutions accountable. The new law will profoundly change how government works in Nigeria. Now we can use the oxygen of information and knowledge to breathe life into governance. It will no longer be business as usual."

The machinery was finally in place for public oversight of government actions. The bill was regarded as a means to blow the lid off theft on a scale that was shocking even by Nigerian standards. With increased scrutiny, more corruption cases were being reported and documented. The level of fraud has not necessarily increased during the Jonathan administration but the number of crimes reported has almost doubled.

As a result, the average Nigerian now has a much greater awareness of corruption. Five years ago, the main platforms for reducing opaqueness were high-level ones such as the Extractive Industries Transparency Initiative, which conducted a series of audits of the oil sector. Now citizen-led projects are pushing for increased transparency. BudgIT, the "civic start-up" behind a mobile and web-based app, converts government budgets into easily understandable charts. Integrity Nigeria, an NGO that promotes transparency in the public and private sectors, has launched egunjedotinfo, a website for reporting bribery.

The FoI bill soon became a double-edged sword for Jonathan and his administration. Suddenly everything was on public display, and material made available thanks to the powers introduced by the new bill became a big weapon for the opposition to steer away scrutiny from themselves. All new revelations that were reported were blamed on Jonathan and his ministers. The public was taking issue with everything from the President's food allowance and government travel budgets to the cost of planting shrubs at the Aso rock presidential villa in Abuja.

With improved means of communication and a rapidly growing social media, the consciousness of the Nigerian people was awakened. But, with many of the media outlets in the hands of Jonathan's opponents the message was quickly hijacked. In January 2012 Jonathan's political honeymoon came to an abrupt halt with the removal of the controversial petrol subsidies. He was portrayed as a President who had campaigned as a man of the people, only to betray them once in power. This was a mantra that was repeated over and over again by his opponents during the demonstrations that followed.

It proved to be a turning point in Jonathan's Presidency. Suddenly people were angry. A little over six months after Jonathan had been sworn in, protesters in Lagos were carrying around mock coffins bearing his name. The powerful elite and opposition forces capitalised on this sentiment and allegations in the media ranged from the bizarre to the wildly exaggerated. "The President's body language seems to be encouraging corrupt practices in the country," said the Speaker of the House of Representatives, Aminu Tambuwal.[4]

"The present administration of President Goodluck Jonathan has been described as the most corrupt in the history of Nigeria," said Executive Secretary of the Anti-corruption Network and former member of the House of Representatives, the Hon Dino Melaye.

The reality is that successive governments before Jonathan had tried, and failed, to deregulate fuel imports. Removing the $8 billion-a-year subsidy – worth more than the combined 2012 budgets for health, education, housing and social protection – was a key part of Jonathan's plan to reform an economy struggling under mounting public debt and declining foreign reserves. Apart from the cost, which was greatly inflated by corruption, the subsidy on imported fuel also discouraged private investment in local refineries. According to one veteran consultant: "You don't need to be a rocket scientist or a forensic accountant to see that wealth generated by oil and gas in Nigeria hasn't always gone to where it should go. But equally this is a problem that started well before Jonathan was inaugurated."

The old system was rife with abuse and fraud with several companies habitually inflating their subsidy claims and obtaining payment without ever having delivered fuel. Inevitably, such graft has an effect on foreign companies doing business. "We have seen a significant increase in concern on the part of companies looking to do business in Nigeria and other countries in the region about governance issues," says one analyst working with international companies and financial institutions that operate in Nigeria. "[This is] not so much because anything has changed in Nigeria but because of greater scrutiny by the regulatory authorities in the US and parts of Europe."[5]

Jonathan's administration further revealed that the chief beneficiaries of the scheme were in fact the 100-odd companies owned by Nigeria's richest people. However, most Nigerians thought cheap fuel was the only benefit they received from living in an oil-rich country and so they were furious. Despite promises of safety nets to protect the poor and the need for new infrastructure and for improvements to the ragged electricity supply, Nigerians feared that the money saved by cutting fuel subsidies would only be swallowed up by political fat-cats.

And so the proposal to remove the fuel subsidy on January 1, 2012, resulted in widespread protests – tagged 'Occupy Nigeria' – across the country, forcing Jonathan to partially reinstate the subsidy. The country's two main trade unions called a strike to demand that the old price be reinstated. The action saw shops, banks and businesses shut, with tens of thousands of people attending the demonstrations. "During the demonstrations, champagne was served, musicians were playing, water was handed out, that doesn't happen by itself," said one Nigerian journalist ruefully. "It was a very well funded operation by those who stood to benefit. Ordinary Nigerians were genuinely unhappy with the removal of the subsidies. But people who knew better did not help. They made it worse because they got worried they would lose out if the subsidies were removed. If they would have come together people would not have demonstrated like they did."

Jonathan's political allies only criticised him for the way the reforms were introduced – the implementation was too abrupt and too big a strain on the average Nigerian's life – but not for the necessity of the policy.

"It was bound to be an unpopular decision and the easy way out – and a safe re-election ticket – would have been to keep them in place," said the journalist. "Jonathan stood firm during two weeks of national uprisings, that is not a sign of weakness."

According to a former bank chairman in Nigeria: "Of course it would have been better to have removed the subsidy completely. But it was still a battle worth fighting. Had there not been an agreement at least to raise prices, there would have huge pressure on public finances. The cost of maintaining the old prices would have had very damaging consequences. It was not the ideal outcome, but Nigeria's economy was on sounder footing after the stand-off than before it began."

Jeffrey D. Sachs, the Nobel prize-winning economist and director of the Earth Institute at Columbia University, expressed a similar view: "The fury at the government's removal of the oil subsidies has been huge, with strikes, violence and political uproar. The removal of subsidies creates short-term pain for many social groups, and considerable short-term fear. The government's actions are easy targets of the political opposition. The public understandably frets that the government might simply steal the budget savings, since governments have stolen so much of the oil wealth in the past.

"The fears of corruption are absolutely understandable, but glimmers of hope — that this time will be different — are also in the air. When Nigeria won relief on its external debt in the mid-2000s, the savings on debt service were actually redirected to meaningful social investments in the states and local governments. The government is now promising to turn the outlays on subsidies into outlays on specific and closely monitored investments in health care, infrastructure, job training and other areas.

"If the president and his team carry through on their plans for bold, honest, equitable and transparent reforms, they are well placed to usher in a new day for Nigeria. Scepticism is running high, but so too are cautious hopes that finally, this decade, Nigeria will join the ranks of the world's most dynamic emerging economies."[6]

Meanwhile, the Finance Minister who saw her 85-year old mother kidnapped because she had spoken out against corruption believes that political transparency and judicial accountability are the priorities to eradicate the disease. And she is backed by financial analysts. "The difficulty is likely to be in the implementation of those plans," says Razia Khan, Head of Africa Research at Standard Chartered. "There is a sense that... if it can't be done by Ngozi, then it is unlikely to be achieved by anyone."[7]

Chapter Seven

THE FACEBOOK PRESIDENT

When Barack Obama announced that he was going to run for the US presidency in 2007, he did so in the same way American politicians have done it for generations: from a platform erected in a town square. When Goodluck Jonathan announced his decision to stand for president on September 16, 2010, he did so in a way no major world leader had ever done before. He took to Facebook.

In a statement to his 217,000 Facebook friends entitled "Declaration of Intent For The 2011 Presidential Race", Jonathan wrote: "Today, I confirm that after wide and thorough consultations spanning the six geo-political zones that make up Nigeria, with members of my family, my party, the opposition, civil society, the Private Sector, members of the Labour Unions, religious leaders, youths and student groups and our revered traditional institutions, I Goodluck Ebele Jonathan by the grace of God hereby offer myself and my services to the Nigerian people as a candidate for the office of President in the forth coming 2011 elections. In presenting myself for service, I make no pretense (sic) that I have a magic wand that will solve all of Nigeria's problems or that I am the most intelligent Nigerian.

"I make no pretense that I have a magic wand that will solve all of Nigeria's problems or that I am the most intelligent Nigerian — far from it," Jonathan's message read. "What I do promise is this — if I am elected president in 2011, I will make a covenant with you, the Nigerian people, to always do right by you, to tell you the truth at all times, to carry you along and most importantly to listen to you, fellow citizens in our communities and also those of you on this page."[1]

Within 24 hours, more than 4,000 followers had "liked" his announcement.[2] In an era when a video demonstration of how to make a loom band can attract more than 20 million views on YouTube, this is a relatively paltry number and many were surprised at Jonathan's decision to use Facebook as a launch-pad for his candidacy, especially given Nigeria's low level of internet connectivity. In a country of 170 million people, there were only 24 million internet users at the end of 2009. Of these, only 980,000 were on Facebook. While this represented Africa's biggest internet market, as well as the continent's largest Facebook user-base, the numbers only accounted for a small proportion of the overall electorate.[3]

So it would be disingenuous to suggest that Jonathan leaves the leader of the free world in the shade when it comes to exploiting the power of social media and the internet as a whole. After all, Obama's stump speech to hundreds of cheering supporters in Springfield, Illinois, immediately reached a much wider audience. It was broadcast live by all the major US TV networks to tens of millions of viewers, was running on newspaper websites within minutes if not seconds of delivery and going viral on Facebook, Twitter and other online platforms with similar speed.

But as the celebrated Canadian philosopher Marshall McLuhan famously said: "The medium is the message". By using social media to make his announcement, Jonathan – the first Nigerian leader to have a Facebook page – was making a hugely significant symbolic gesture. Internet penetration in Nigeria grew by 12 per cent from 2000 to 2009, and most Facebook users on Facebook are between the ages of 13 and 25.[4] The potential audience might have been too small to justify a grand Obama-style social media campaign, but by opting for Facebook as the medium for his message, Jonathan became a trailblazer in African politics. It also ingratiated him with a key and growing constituency: Nigeria's increasingly politically aware population of young people. Not surprisingly, perhaps, they voted for him overwhelmingly.[5] [6]

By March 2011, less than a month before his first presidential election, Jonathan had more followers on Facebook than nearly all the world's leading heads of state. His official Facebook page had attracted more than half a million "likes". That was more thumbs-ups than the British Prime Minister David Cameron, German Chancellor Angela Merkel, Canada PM Stephen Harper, Italy's former Prime Minister Silvio Berlusconi and South Africa's President Jacob Zuma, combined. At the time he even had more fans than the entire British Royal Family. In fact, Jonathan came second only to US President Barack Obama who – at that time – had received 18.7 million "likes".

"I have not experienced any election where the youth feel

personally involved until this one," said Dalhatu Sarki Tafida, director-general of the Jonathan campaign in 2011. "These ideas of Facebook and Internet access were alien to us, but young people are embracing them. On the day of the declaration, we were in contact with 20 million of them. I never thought we would be like the Americans."[7]

A Campaign Manager during the presidential race said:

"It was really a genuine organic campaign. At a time when we pump so much money into social media for every election, even creating a 'following', this was for real. People in Nigeria and abroad just caught on to this. It was crazy. There was no top-down megaphone barking out orders. This thing just grew. The President was actually responding to posts himself, he was actually reading what they wrote. I think he was as excited about this as the people who received his responses were. I can't emphasize enough the important impact this movement had on a young and growing democracy. People felt involved, like what they were saying mattered. There was a real excitement. He posted something and immediately he got thousands of responses. This was not just a gimmick. This sh*t was real. We were part of that, it was big.

"It was definitely a feeling that a new era of leadership had begun, and that the old guard was gone. Someone posted and suggested that Nigeria should open a consulate in San Francisco, which has a large Nigerian community. The President read that post and then he came to us and said 'I like this idea, and I think it would open up the West Coast. I want us to look into this.' And so we did, and now a Nigerian Consulate has opened in San Francisco. Tell me somewhere else in the world where that happens? Young people in Nigeria have a direct line to their President. That's quite powerful.

"The President's page is not all praise. He receives a lot of criticism. I remember the whole debacle with their football team being banned, the Eagles. There was an outcry of protests on his page. In the end he re-evaluated his decision and the ban was lifted. So it's not just that he looks at the good stuff, the easy things. No, he actually reads it to understand his electorate. What they care about. The social media campaign has definitely opened him up to a lot of criticism. I mean they can just write what they want on his page. They can say things about their President that they could never do before. That's not all good for Jonathan. But this is democracy and he believes in it, there is no going back

"The whole social media campaign has given us an enormous amount of information that before did not 'exist' in Nigeria. It has certainly helped in better understanding the electorate. Not just the big issues, we know about those, but what really matters to young people on a different level. Not just now, but what they want in life."

Ken Banks, founder of kiwanja.net, an information technology site that provides support for NGOs, reckons that the calibre of Internet users is key. Given that people with access to the web tend to be in urban areas, with an above average level of literacy and relatively prosperous they are something of a goldmine for the ambitious politician. "What you have to bear in mind is that there is a critical minority of opinion leaders on Facebook, including local business CEOs, young activists, and university graduates," he says.

"EnoughisEnough Nigeria"(EIE), a group that is driving a youth voter-registration campaign, also recognises Jonathan's shrewdness in prioritising young people and forcing other candidates to follow suit. "Young people are more aware of the issues, more concerned about the country and angry about the state of the nation," says EIE co-founder Chude Jideonwo.[8] He notes that Jonathan's surprise Facebook announcement was made at the same time that one of his main presidential rivals, former military ruler Ibrahim Babangida, entered the contest: "Many people believe this was a strategic move to overshadow Babangida's announcement and, if it was, frankly it worked."

It is this direct and personal form of interaction that is calculated to endear Jonathan to his country's growing young and web-savvy electorate. Today the president is making extensive use of Facebook, on which he has more than 375,000 followers and more than 1.5 million likes, and understands the importance of being proactive. Jonathan's Facebook page is regularly updated and his advisors track feedback from followers and other users. He has even been known to take to the site in person and respond to comments. On one occasion, he wrote: "Again I spent time reading your comments and yesterday a youth named Toyin Dawodu indicated that he had an idea for a project that could deliver 4,000 MWs of electricity... Toyin, someone from my office will make contact with you regarding your idea. I know I can not attend to every comment or suggestion due to time constraints, but please do know that I read them and they influence my actions."

Naturally, not all feedback is positive. "We are tired of rhetoric, what we need is action," wrote one commentator in response to a post concerning Nigeria's frequent power shortages. This is an illustration of how Jonathan's engagement with social media offers him another dividend: a means to monitor national sentiment. "The President has opened up a new channel of popular involvement in Nigerian politics, encouraging young people to feel like they have a voice," says EIE's Jideonwo. "This can only be a good thing."

Nor does the president ignore Twitter. In this, of course, he is not alone, according to twiplomacy.com, a subsidiary of the global public relations and communications network Burson-Marsteller. It calculated that by mid-2014 world leaders had sent 1.9 million tweets and had 157 million followers between them.

The boom in social media and internet-use as a whole is just one strand of a wider revolution that is taking place in Nigerian society as people adjust to a changing media landscape. Elsewhere in the cultural sphere, film-making has become big business. Just as Hollywood gave the US homegrown entertainment and Bollywood did the same for India, so Nollywood is now entertaining not just Nigeria but West Africa as a whole. Indeed, the Nigerian movie business was recently valued at $5.1 billion, making it the third biggest film industry in the world after India and the US. If you rank it in terms of the number of productions completed per year, it leapfrogs the US to second place.

While it has become more sophisticated in recent years, with a growing number of international co-productions raising standards, Nollywood very definitely has its roots in the beliefs and preoccupations of the Nigerian villager. "If Hollywood's forte is jaw-dropping spectacle and Bollywood's is heart-warming musical slush, then Nollywood's special draw is a genre that might be described as the voodoo horror flick: films that revolve around witchcraft and demonic possession," Jeevan Vasager wrote in an in-depth report for UK newspaper The Guardian in 2006.

The film generally recognised as the father of this genre is Living In Bondage. Made in 1992, its plot centres on a variation of the Faustian pact: a man joins a cult, sacrifices his wife in return for vast riches but is then haunted by her ghost. The audience certainly got their money's worth. This straight-to-video classic lasts a marathon two hours and 43 minutes and it certainly had all the ingredients of what proved to be a winning formula.

"The movies can be read as fantasies," Vasagar wrote. "They allow the powerless to feel vicariously powerful. The stories tell of poor men getting rich, of errant husbands who find their penises shrinking, of love rivals who go blind or crazy and end up running naked and shrieking into the streets. There is the occasional humorous twist. One classic features a controlling girlfriend who miniaturises her man and traps him inside a bottle. But the films always end with the practitioners of witchcraft being punished (although sometimes they are redeemed by finding Jesus) and the virtuous being rewarded.

"One of the reasons this is such a powerful draw is that in Nigeria, as elsewhere in Africa, Christianity lies like a veneer over much older beliefs. The occult movies give people a chance to thrill once again to the power of the old religion, but then celebrate the victory of the new faith as the credits roll."

While the first Nollywood films were produced using celluloid and Living In Bondage and many of its successors made using video technology, it was the advent of high-definition digital filming and editing technology in the late 90s that kicked production into overdrive. The majority of the estimated 2,000 Nigerian movies released annually are made by independent film-makers using personal digital cameras on shoestring budgets. Many are made on a budget of around $20,000 and are completed in less than a week but go on to sell tens of thousands of copies on DVD. It was in a bid to raise production standards that Jonathan pledged to create a $200 million loan fund to finance film projects in 2010.

Apart from selling in Nigerian shops and market stalls, Nollywood films also find a market among the Nigerian diaspora in Europe, North America and the Caribbean. While the biggest sellers tend to be made in English, there is also a market for films made in Hausa, Yoruba, Ibo, Edo and other languages that have a significant number of speakers.

A sign that the Nigerian movie business is coming of age culturally as well as commercially came in 2013 when a Nigerian-British co-production of Half Of A Yellow Sun, Chimamanda Ngozi Adichie's bestselling novel revolving around the Biafran War, went on general release. With a budget of $8 million, which is said to make it the most expensive Nigerian movie ever made, it was filmed on location in Nigeria in Calabar and Creek Town. It also had one of the most starry line-ups ever assembled for a Nollwood film, with the leading roles taken by Chiwetel Ejiofor – who was nominated for a Best Actor Oscar for his role in 12 Years A Slave – and Thandie Newton. "The future of Nigerian film is very good," the movie's Nigerian-born director Biyi Bandele said. "There are many young filmmakers right now out there. Some of them have grown up within the Nollywood tradition, others have gone to film school and you just have this mix of talent (and) lots of voices and I'm really excited."

Just as the future looks bright for the big screen, it does for the small screen too. Television is another area of the Nigerian media that is undergoing a renaissance. It was an entirely state-run business until 1992 when deregulation was introduced. This quickly led to a proliferation of private TV companies who offered competition to the government station NTV (later NTA) for the first time. But the real gamechanger came in 1994 when Digital Satellite Television DStv entered the market as Nigeria's first pay TV company. A subsidiary of South Africa's MultiChoice, the leading satellite TV operator in sub-Saharan Africa, it soon became the dominant player in the Nigerian market thanks to first-mover advantage and superior production values to those of the competition.

Frontage Satellite Television (FStv) became the first indigenous pay TV operator in 2004 but, within a few years, it and a number of other entrants to the market went out of business after proving unable to survive in the face of intense competition. While Nigerian stations are active in the cable sector, the pay TV market is dominated to this day by DStv and Star TV, part of China's StarTimes group. Star has successfully targeted the lower income segment of the market and invested $94 million in its Nigerian offering over the course of 2013. Meanwhile, MultiChoice extended its domination with the launch of GOtv, a station that allows for mobile and handheld viewing.

It is estimated that the Nigerian TV business has attracted $1 billion of private-sector investment over the years and created thousands of jobs. Apart from employment opportunities in TV stations, the advertising industry has undergone considerable expansion, with Nigerian businesses increasingly using domestically-owned agencies to shoot and edit TV commercials.

A number of impediments to growth persist, however. Apart from the ongoing problems caused for both broadcasters and consumers by the absence of a reliable power supply, piracy and an associated unwillingness by foreign content owners to sell on rights remain thorny issues.

These difficulties are not insurmountable, according to the South Africa-based African Business Review. "Infrastructure development, tighter legislation and stronger regulatory frameworks would go a long way to addressing these issues, but the initiative should not just lie with government," it reported in March 2013. "High quality Nigerian-produced TV can itself do much to challenge the negative perceptions that deter business. More international broadcasting in a similar vein to that of African Independent Television (AIT) in Lagos and Minaj Broadcast International (MBI) in Obosi – both of which transmit to a global audience – would go a long way towards bridging the divide between Nigeria and the rest of the world. Such channels present an opportunity to showcase the growing expertise of Nigerian producers and to reflect the best of Nigerian culture."

While television is making progress, print media, once so dominant, appears to be suffering. In 1975, Nigeria's leading newspaper, The Daily Times, was selling 275,000 copies a day during the week and 400,000 copies of its Sunday paper. Following its acquisition by the government in that year, however, its fortunes waned. It was returned to private ownership in 2004 but dogged by allegations of asset-stripping and plagued by legal actions it ceased production in 2011.

Dozens of newspapers survive but quite how well they are doing is hard to judge. In 2011, The Advertisers' Association of Nigeria (ADVANS) published a controversial report on the daily sales figures of 15 newspapers. It contended that the circulation of the bestselling newspaper in the country, Punch, was just 34,264 – far less than the 120-150,000 claimed by its publisher. The Nation was ranked second and The Sun third, with similar discrepancies between the circulations they claimed and the sales figures arrived at by ADVANS. To the anger of their publishers, The Guardian and ThisDay, the two papers believed to have the highest level of advertising revenues, were placed fifth and sixth respectively.

The report's statistics, based on the supply and sales

figures of the country's 45 newspaper distribution centres, were hotly contested by the newspaper owners, who claimed that – among other things – subscription sales were ignored. Nor is an association of advertisers, who can only benefit from a finding that circulations are lower than claimed, a disinterested researcher.

One Western analyst who often travels to Abuja expressed his fascination with the vibrant Nigerian press, "I take the car to work and then when I stop at a the red-light just outside of the Hilton the same newspaper vendor always come up to knock on my window. I buy about seven different newspapers per day, which is a good bunch. At home we are all about online news, losing out on the story behind, but in Nigeria the print press is not dead. No, far from it."

But its headline claim, that the titles sold just 300,000 copies between them, remains a shocking one as it implies that just one Nigerian in 500 buys a daily newspaper. Part of the problem, of course, is illiteracy. Nigeria has the fifth lowest rate of literacy in the world, with only 61 per cent of the population able to read and write, according to the CIA World Factbook. And this makes education a national priority, one that is complicated by the fact that its people are on the move. Like everywhere else in the developing world, Nigeria is experiencing a migration from rural areas to its cities. The population of Lagos, for example, currently nudging 20 million, is expected to rise to 25 million by 2025, making it the third biggest city in the world after Tokyo and Mumbai. Already, one out of two Nigerians lives in an urban area and towns and cities are growing at a rate of 3.5 per cent a year.

Meanwhile, it is experiencing a population explosion, which is predicted to take the total number of Nigerians from today's level of 170 million to over 200 million by the year 2020, as reported by Nigeria's National Population Commission. As every demographer knows, a fast-growing population is a young population. According to the UN, 44 per cent of Nigeria's population was below the age of 14 in 2010 and the CIA World Factbook puts the median age at 17.9.

In this context, education certainly becomes a key issue. Nigeria is perhaps fortunate then in having a president for whom education has been a preoccupation since his days as a politician in his home state of Bayelsa. As Deputy Governor there and then as Vice President under Yar'Adua, education was one of the few portfolios that Jonathan was given meaningful powers to develop. As President he is now beginning to implement his wider ambitions in this area.

Poor families in Nigeria have long had only two options. They can either keep their children at home and put them to work so they can contribute to the family's survival, or send them away to reduce the burden on the family's resources and provide them with some kind of education. If the latter course is possible, most children end up in free boarding schools.

In northern Nigeria, Chad and Niger, there is a type of Quranic schooling called "the Almajiri system of education." An Almajiri is a person who moves from one place to another in search of knowledge. The system originated in northern Nigeria long before the British colonised the country in the 19th century and is credited with having produced generations of regional leaders, religious reformers clerics, administrators and scholars. Under British rule, however, the Almajiri education system was more or less eradicated. Funding to all Islamic schools was halted and they were replaced by institutions that promoted a Western system of education. Religious madrassas were neglected and left to be managed by individuals who were often not qualified to fulfil such a role and used their status to pursue personal agendas. In the end, the Almajiri system was marked by a lack of regulation and accountability. Meanwhile, children sent to these schools – separated as they were from their families and communities, with virtually no means of maintaining contact – were left particularly reliant on their mallams and fellow students. What's more, the majority of these children came from poor families and, as students were required to pay their teachers, many were sent on to the streets to beg for money and food in order to cover their costs. The Almajiri system has now degenerated to such an extent that the very word "Almajiri" has become more associated with child beggars than students. As a result, Almajiris tend to find themselves with few job prospects or any kind of support once they have completed their "education".

The curriculum at these schools has traditionally been built around studying Arabic and the Quran, but during the last decade extremist philosophies have been gaining a foothold. Radical clerics have been teaching students to hate everything that is Western or influenced by it, including the

Federal government. As an estimated eight to 10 million children live in Almajiri schools in Nigeria, this has become a serious problem.

One of the organised radical groupings that has stepped in to fill the vacuum, of course, is Boko Haram. It is thought that it now draws most of its recruits from those who grew up under the Almajiri system, some motivated by religious belief and others by simple material necessity. Boko Haram's objective is to eradicate western influence and implement its own interpretation of Shari'a across Nigeria. This is why it targets secular and Islamic schools alike across the north-eastern part of the country. Boko Haram has been attacking Islamiyya schools, for example, which are similar to the Almajiri schools in their Islamic teaching but also draw inspiration from Western educational models.

In an attempt to tackle the root of the problem the Jonathan administration has initiated a state-run Almajiri Education Programme. This is an attempt to take the Almajiri system into the mainstream by complementing traditional Islamic studies with basic education in mathematics, science, and English. The federal government guarantees funding for the building of schools and accommodation; the provision of equipment, furnishings and textbooks; the designing of the curriculum; and the provision of the necessary training for teachers. Once established, these schools are handed over to the control of state governments and are monitored to ensure compliance with minimum academic standards for basic education. A total of 125 boarding and day schools have been constructed during the last four years.

In addition, twelve new universities have been built since 2011; nine in the north and three in the south. The Girl-Child Education and Back to School initiatives have been launched; enrolment in basic school has increased from 23 million in 2010 to 29 million in 2012, and enrolment to university has gone up by 20 per cent between 2011 and 2013. Since 2007 the Federal Government has almost tripled the budget allocation for education from N224 billion to N634 billion.

But Nigeria is a big country and, given the state of neglect into which education had been allowed to fall, there is much left to do. Of the estimated 57 million young people worldwide who are not receiving a formal education, around 10 million live in Nigeria. The majority of non-attendees are girls, mainly in the majority-Muslim north, but out-of-school boys are then often recruited into terrorist ranks, perpetuating a cycle of poverty and instability. The abduction of more than 200 schoolgirls in Chibok, Borno state, in early 2014 highlighted the increasing ferocity with which Boko Haram is targeting schools in its north-eastern stronghold. According to an Amnesty International report in October 2013, around seventy teachers and more than a hundred school children have lost their lives. In Yobe state, which had been in a state of emergency for nearly a year by mid-2014, 209 schools have been destroyed. In Borno state more than 800 classrooms have been burned down.

Jonathan is determined to neutralise the threat from Boko Haram and, while he does not see education as a panacea for Nigeria's security problems, he believes that giving the millions of children vulnerable to such groups a proper formal schooling would be a significant step forward in tackling militancy in the country.

A key figure involved in carrying out this policy is Fatima Akilu, the Director of Behavioural Analysis and Strategic Communication at the Office of the National Security Adviser. A psychologist by training, she began her career in the UK at Birmingham University and the Birmingham Mental Health Trust, where she looked at pathways into care for Asian, blacks and whites. Akilu then moved to New York to work as a forensic psychologist at a new purpose-built centre for sex offenders in New York state. On returning to Nigeria, where psychology is not a mainstream profession, she started to work on the Millennium Development Goals programme. "It was really a blessing," she says, "because I learnt all about development, which is an important component in my job today."

After writing a series of children's books to illustrate the Millennium Development Goals for a younger audience, Akilu started a publishing company and became chairman of the Nigerian daily newspaper Leadership. It was at a meeting of the editorial boards of national newspapers that Akilu first met her future boss, the National Security Adviser General Andrew Azazi. He was clearly impressed by the psychology graduate turned sex-crime specialist, with a development focus, and asked her to join his team. Her current boss, Colonel Sambo Dasuki, has continued to retain confidence in her work.

Akilu duly joined the Department of State Services, one of very few women on the team and its only psychologist. "I began to study the behaviours of Boko Haram, their motivation, their narratives," she says. "Actually everything that I had done then came together. I needed to understand the media because Boko Haram uses the media very effectively and we needed to make the counter-narratives. They gave me the time and resources to really study the problem and come up with a framework to tackle the situation. I visited a lot of the countries affected by Boko Haram and I felt that the best approach was a three-pronged approach which would look at de-radicalising terrorists and terror suspects, and then the middle bit which is about community commitment and building resilience within communities, providing post trauma counselling for victims that had been affected by terrorism, and enabling structures where you connect traditional rulers with Government officials and NGOs, working together for peace. The third approach I felt we needed to have a strategic communication proponent. What are they saying, what are they using to support what they are saying and how could we use those same things to produce counter-narratives."

In 2011, Akilu started Nigeria's first Countering Violent Extremism (CVE) programme, a revolutionary concept not only in Nigeria, but worldwide. The UK, for example, does not have a CVE programme but is now looking at starting up one. The two countries may operate in very different contexts but as more attacks originate from within the UK the government is beginning to dedicate resources to preventative CVE programmes.

On 20 March 2014 the National Security Adviser, who unveiled the programme, said its strategy was arrived at only after a rigorous examination of the root causes of terrorism. "What we have learnt is that there is not one particular path that leads to terrorism, rather, there are many often complicated paths," he said. "The programme seeks to prevent attacks before they happen by preventing our people from becoming terrorists in the first place. The soft approach to counter terrorism has resulted in the development of a Countering Violent Extremism (CVE) programme that is vertical and involves the three tiers of government: federal, state and local. The programme is also horizontal, involving civil societies, academics, traditional, religious and community leaders."[9]

For her part, Akilu argues that combating violent extremism effectively in the long term involves having "an education system that prepares the students for a purpose, and then allows for critical thinking to be used for this purpose, but also in life at large." After many years of decay, she argues, Nigeria's education system has failed to fulfil either of these criteria.

"Education must be more than just academics," she says. "There are lots of other things that really make you who you are today. Some of these things are so implicit for those that have been fortunate enough to have access to it that they don't realise their impact. It has been imbedded in the education system that you have been privileged to have. Like 'critical thinking and logical reasoning.' Something that you may be taught from primary school but a lot of schools in Nigeria doesn't have that because over the years the education system has degraded to such a level. So those are things that we are trying to teach teachers. We are trying to teach them how to teach in an imaginative way, because a child and an education without imagination is only half as good as it could be. You can teach a child science, but he needs to have the imagination to know what to do with it, how to apply it. A child needs to have the knowledge to say no to terrorism."

These measures, by their very nature, will take time to pay off. The benefits from them will be reaped not by the administration that introduced them but by generations to come. As a result, Akilu's role is in some ways an unrewarding job with few short-term successes for the media to celebrate. It is also one that requires her to stand her ground in a male-dominated department more accustomed to taking a hard line on such issues rather than championing "soft" approaches such as the one she is promoting.

"CVE is by its very nature about changing processes, changing institutions, changing people, changing behaviours, so it is more of a generational work," she says. "You will need a generation of practitioners, peace workers, a generation of people who think differently before you will see real change. You need to make changes in all layers of society, social, economic, national identity. There are many, many different things that you would have to change and that takes time. But there are some quick wins within that. For example, some of the changes within education, where we now see more sports, more arts, ways to enable critical thinking, and that are reforms that we can install relatively quickly. So the platforms can be developed in relatively short terms but you are not going to see massive impacts immediately. But CVE has to be like that by its very nature because it is about preventing a generation of young children from taking up arms against the state. It's about breaking a vicious cycle.

"It is a particularly difficult area to measure because there are so many moving parts all the time. It is hard to know whether it is your intervention that has prevented someone from taking up arms, to join terrorism. Because here success translates into preventing someone. In some ways we may never have a direct causal link to show for. But that might not be the overall point anyway. Our goal is to engage with youth and to give them an alternative. We do have a team that uses a lot of the indices from the development filed to measure improvements in people's life. So we are borrowing from some existing models to come up with ways of measuring and to try and come up with our own. But this is a pilot programme; there will have to be some trial and error as we'll go along.

"My job is to make sure that this is not a one-man show. The structures must be in place to continue after this administration and my mandate. The best way is to go through existing institutions. Part of CVE is actually about building up institutions, because they are the best places to carry out this job long-term. Then we can exit because the capability is there. It is not particularly headline grabbing, because a lot of the work is about building structures. But there is a programme and there is a plan."

The shocking nature of the Chibok kidnappings has tended to overshadow everything else when it comes to discussion of the Boko Haram issue, but Aliku hopes that her work can shed light on the wider issues involved and allow Nigeria to move forward with the help of the next generation.

"Everyone just wants to talk about Chibok, and I do understand," she says. "Many things made Chibok into what it was. The sheer audacity of taking so many girls. Also that these girls were sitting their exams for their next stage in their life. And the fact that they were taken alive. There were so many other girls that were all slaughtered, they never even got the chance. With Chibok there is a hope, which has been galvanized.

"But these horrors won't be solved when the girls come back. We need to solve them together and we have a long-term plan, because there are no quick fixes. That won't solve anything. Young people matter in Nigeria. They are the ones who can bring us forward. What we need to do is to build the institutions that will allow them to progress"

A measure of the relative progress of modernising Nigeria's institutions in recent years was borne out by how it reacted to the deadly Ebola virus.

In July 2014, Patrick Sawyer, a consultant for the Liberian Ministry of Finance, arrived in Nigeria but collapsed at Lagos airport. He was immediately detained by health authorities and rushed to a quarantine Nigerian hospital, suspecting that he might be carrying the deadly and untreatable Ebola virus. Soon after Sawyer died from Ebola, but only after health workers who treated him had contracted the virus. Officials estimated that he had come into contact with 59 people on his travels. Ebola had arrived in Nigeria.

This outbreak, which began in March 2014 in Guinea, has claimed more than 1,000 lives and infected over a thousand more across West Africa. Many who live in the region have been deeply confused about what Ebola is and how to prevent it. Resistance and denial run high, and local culture is a challenge in communities where world events are seen through the prism of religious fatalism and superstition.

Conspiracy theories and variations of the same rumour circulated throughout Nigeria: that drinking water wells were being poisoned by the government in order to cash in on the international aid meant for addressing the crisis. The gossip surrounding the Ebola disease stoked an existing paranoia that the lives of ordinary Africans were expendable. And an exodus by foreign aid workers triggered feelings of wartime abandonment and that NGOs were more concerned about their insurance and image than the people.

But the misconception of the virus is not limited to Africa. "We apologize, but due to the Ebola virus, we are not accepting Africans at the moment," read a notice at a bar in Seoul, South Korea. This sign was photographed and soon went viral. The Daily Beast reported that in Italy some schools had warned that pupils of African origin would require additional health certification before returning to school; something which was not deemed necessary for white pupils who may have travelled to Africa over the summer holidays.

The deadly virus revived stereotypes and clichés of life in Africa. "In palpable ways, Ebola has allowed for the 'dark continent' narrative to re-emerge, if it ever really disappeared", wrote Fungai Machirori, a blogger who runs Zimbabwe's first web-based platform for women, Her Zimbabwe. "And in its inclusivity, Africa is collapsed into one territory, one country, one race. Through these short-cut understandings emerges a dominant global hysteria that lends itself to racial profiling and generalisations that make me wonder just how far, if at all, the discourse around blackness has progressed".[10]

When Ebola reached the densely-populated city of Lagos (21 million people at the last count) there was deep concern. After all, outbreaks of the disease usually occur in more remote areas, and Patrick Sawyer was the first victim of the virus travelling by air.

However, the spread of Ebola requires contact with bodily fluids – making the untreatable virus possible to contain. "The risk of infection for travellers is very low", stated the World Health Organisation. In general, health-care workers treating patients with the disease, mourners of Ebola victims who come into direct contact with the body and family members of infected patients, are at the greatest risk for infection themselves. And proportionately, there are more deadly diseases. By August 2014, a total of 1,427 people across Nigeria, Guinea, Liberia and Sierra Leone had died of the viral disease. By comparison, the "Swine" flu pandemic of 2009-10 killed over 16,000 people.

As soon as the news of Sawyer's arrival reached the Nigerian health authorities the country was put on high alert. Within days specifically designed "disease isolation centres" – the setting up of secure holding rooms where any potential cases would be isolated – at international airports across the country were put in place. At airports, seaports and land border crossings, health officials were distributing information. And the new academic year, due to start on 1 September 2014, was pushed forward and all schools in Nigeria were ordered to be shut until 13 October to allow for staff to be trained on how to handle suspected Ebola cases.

As of August 2014, there were 16 reported cases of Ebola. Five of those infected by Sawyer later died, while seven recovered and were discharged from the isolation centre in Lagos, including two nurses. All of the 129 people who were on the same flight as Sawyer were placed under medical surveillance and completed the 21 day observation incubation period. Only one person was found to be symptomatic and is still being observed and remains in isolation.

The containment of the disease by a country of 170 million people, many living in densely packed communities, was a remarkable achievement and praised by the United Nations.

David Navarro, a Special Envoy of the United Nations Secretary-General, who had visited Liberia, Guinea and Sierra Leone, the countries worst hit by Ebola before coming to Nigeria, told Jonathan that he had come, on the instruction of the UN Secretary-General, to applaud Nigeria's containment of the virus.

"The Secretary-General asked me to come here too, not because you have an Ebola problem, but because you have tackled it in an exemplary fashion. Your personal leadership on the matter has been key. There may still be some work to be done before the virus is completely cleared out from here, but other countries can learn from your fine example," said Navarro.[11]

The Ebola outbreak could have been so much worse and it was another sign that Nigeria appears to be finally living up to its potential.

Chapter Eight

OUT OF AFRICA

On 23 August 2011 – with the popular insurrection against
the Libyan leader Muammar Gaddafi at its height – Professor
Viola Onwuliri, Nigeria's Minister of State for Foreign Affairs,
held a press conference in Abuja. She told reporters that the
rebel-led National Transitional Council (NTC) in Libya was
"the legitimate representative of the Libyan people" and added
that Gaddafi, the country's leader of 41 years, should
relinquish power immediately. Given subsequent events, this
might at first sight appear to be an unremarkable episode in
African history but it was, in fact, a moment of considerable
significance. Up to that point South Africa was the country
to which the rest of the continent looked for leadership in
international affairs. In breaking ranks with Pretoria and its
allies in the African Union (AU), Nigeria asserted its
independence and proved that it was prepared to make a
stand without the support of Africa's traditional powerbroker-
in-chief.

South Africa's response was immediate, and there were
insinuations that Nigeria was an acolyte of the west. "Nigeria
is jumping the gun in recognizing the rebels as representatives
of Libya," Gwede Mantashe, secretary-general of South

Africa's ruling African National Congress, told reporters in Johannesburg later that day. "The AU position stays." This confrontation between two long-time partners was watched with great interest by diplomatic commentators. One American analyst said: "If Nigeria and South Africa are indeed the two 'African superpowers,' South Africa may feel threatened by Nigeria taking the initiative in this fashion. South Africa may fear that other countries will soon follow Nigeria's lead, which would make the AU a follower, and not a forger, of the African stance on Libya."

While the AU had expressed "deep concern" over the violence in Libya, saying it posed "a serious threat to peace and security in that country and in the region as a whole, as well as to the safety and dignity of Libyans and of the migrant workers, notably the African ones living in Libya", South Africa did not follow Nigeria's lead on recognising the NTC until late September, a full month after Professor Onwuliri's statement. This delay can be attributed in large part to the deep bonds between Gaddafi and South Africa, including former President Nelson Mandela, and a reluctance by the ruling ANC to be seen to be doing the work of the "imperialist" western powers.

The Libyan leader had played an historic role in supporting South Africa's liberation struggle against the apartheid regime by supplying the African National Congress's armed wing, Umkhonto we Sizwe, with weapons, money and training. In recognition of this, Mandela made a controversial visit to Gaddafi following his release from prison in 1990. Despite the Libyan strongman's pariah status at that time thanks to the downing of PanAm Flight 103 in 1988, Mandela awarded him the Order of Good Hope, South Africa's highest award for a foreigner. While this made Pretoria's caution understandable, it did nothing to detract from the symbolism of Nigeria's stand. Just as the rebasing of Nigeria's GDP affected the way the country was seen in economic terms, Abuja's leadership on the Libyan question changed the way it was perceived in diplomatic terms.

The tension between South Africa and Nigeria is especially painful for the Nigerians, who staunchly supported the liberation struggle against apartheid. Monthly contributions were deducted from the salaries of ordinary workers to support the ANC during the long years of exile. In the early part of the century, General Obasanjo and South African President Thabo Mbeki were seen as Africa's foremost statesmen. They worked together to build the African Union and its development and accountability provisions formulated as the New Partnership for Africa's Development (NEPAD). But in recent years Africa's two great powers have had an at times uneasy relationship, reflected in a different outlook on foreign affairs. South Africa, as a member of the BRICS group of emerging nations, leans much more closely towards China and Russia. Nigeria has often been an ally of the West, though by no means an unquestioning one, and played a constructive role both regionally and in the continent as a whole.

While the support for action in Libya was an important moment for the Jonathan administration, it was not out of keeping with the direction that the country had been going for some years. Since Nigeria obtained its independence from

Britain in 1960, the African continent has been the centrepiece of its foreign policy theatre. While Nigeria has not itself been immune to the conflicts in Africa, having fought a devastating civil war, endured years of oppressive governance under successive military regimes, seen oil-based conflict in the Niger Delta, and fought against a bloody insurrection by Boko Haram in the North, the country has long played a leading role in conflict prevention, resolution and management elsewhere on the continent. Successive Nigerian governments, whether autocratic military regimes or civilian democracies, have devoted a great deal of human and material resources to the prevention and resolution of conflicts in Africa.

One of Nigeria's first major continental acts was to champion the creation of the Economic Community of West African States (ECOWAS) in 1975 in the face of opposition from the government of France, which saw it as a potential threat to its power and influence in the region. Not only was this body established by the Treaty of Lagos but its headquarters were located in Abuja. Nigeria has sought to manage inter-state relations among the 15 member countries within the West African sub-region under the framework of ECOWAS ever since, as well as forming bilateral arrangements with their immediate neighbours.

It was the civil war in Liberia that prompted the formation of an associated multilateral armed force in 1990. ECOMOG (the Economic Community of West African States Monitoring Group) was set up with Nigerian armed forces as its backbone and additional units provided by other

ECOWAS members. "Operation Liberty" was planned with the aim of bringing peace and stability to that country after the warlord Charles Taylor's incursion and ensuing civil war overthrew former President Samuel Doe. Following seven years of fighting and resulting in what was deemed a, relatively, free election in which Taylor became President of Liberia, Nigerian forces withdrew.

However, Taylor's support for the murderous Revolutionary United Front in neighbouring Sierra Leone, which led to his indictment for war crimes at the Hague, and the eruption of a new civil war in Liberia, created a fresh crisis in the country that Nigeria was forced to mange. In the end, a deal was brokered in which Taylor agreed to go into exile in Nigeria in return for immunity from prosecution. This agreement was broken by the US, with the backing of the new Liberian government of President Ellen Sirleaf Johnson, and Taylor was shipped off to be prosecuted at the Hague. Obasanjo was livid that the Americans had broken their word, and this incident did much to cloud relations between the two countries.

Meanwhile, the chaos in Liberia had spilled over into its neighbour Sierra Leone after Charles Taylor's National Patriotic Front of Liberia (NPFL) backed the Revolutionary United Front (RUF) in its campaign against the government there. The elected civilian administration, headed by Ahmed Tejan Kabbah, had been in office for just one year, when it was overthrown in a military coup led by Major Johnny Paul Koroma, who had escaped from the prison where he had been held following an earlier attempted coup in September 1996.

Kabbah fled to Conakry in neighbouring Guinea from where he invoked his country's defence pact with ECOMOG. In early 1998, it duly launched Operation Sandstorm in a bid to restore him to power. Within weeks of its troops moving in, the rebels were forced out of the capital Freetown and Kabbah was reinstated as president. It was not long before the rebels regrouped and launched a counter attack, however. An orgy of looting, destruction, abduction, rape and killing ensued and the country was facing the most severe famine threat of any African nation, with as many as half a million in danger of starving, when ECOMOG troops, reinforced by several additional battalions from Nigeria, liberated Freetown after three weeks of intense fighting. A government of national unity was formed, a UN peacekeeping force was installed, and ECOMOG forces – including 12,000 Nigerian soldiers – were withdrawn in March and April 2000. By this point, the civil war had lasted 11 years and left more than 50,000 dead.

The human and financial cost of the intervention in Sierra Leone led many to ask whether it would mark the end of intervention by the regional giant in West Africa's conflicts. At the time Nigeria was returning to democracy under Obasanjo and in severe economic straits after a ruinous 15-year stretch of military rule. Nine years of intervention in Liberia and Sierra Leone had taken a heavy toll on the exchequer and the priority now was to reduce costs.

But even though some in Nigeria were keen to drop what had become a costly burden, many analysts considered this neither likely nor desirable. The then UN Secretary-General

Kofi Annan spoke for many when he visited Nigeria for two days in July 1999 en route to the Organisation of African Unity (OAU) summit in Algiers. "I am here to thank Nigeria for its efforts in the region on peacekeeping and trying to make sure that we are able to calm the waters and settle the crisis in the region from Liberia to Sierra Leone," Annan told reporters during his visit.[1]

Indeed Nigeria reaffirmed its commitment to its role as an African peacemaker just five years later. On August 19, 2004, the Nigerian Senate approved a request by Obasanjo to send up to 1,500 Nigerian troops to Sudan's troubled Darfur region to serve with an African Union (AU) protection force. And this represented a significant commitment: the two battalions of troops that went to Darfur constituted three quarters of the entire 2,000-strong AU peacekeeping force for the region.

Nigeria's engagement with Southern Sudan went back to the advent of the civil war in the early 1980s. The government hosted a series of peace talks between the fractured parties in Lagos, Abuja and Kano in the late 1980s and early 1990s, all intended to facilitate a resolution of the long-raging conflict. In 2004, Obasanjo, in his capacity as chairman of the AU, hosted a round of ultimately successful peace talks in Abuja between the Sudanese government and the two rebel movements in Darfur. These talks laid the foundation for what would later result in the signing of a comprehensive peace accord between the government of Sudan and the Sudan Peoples Liberation Movement (SPLM).

In the years that followed, Nigeria committed both

human and material resources in its effort to reach a long-term solution to the problem. The country organized several meetings under the auspices of the African Union and the United Nations, which resulted in a consensus on the Declaration of Principles between the central Sudanese government and the SPLM that led to self-determination for Southern Sudan. Its status as an independent sovereign state today is the dividend earned from the many peace initiatives advanced by Nigeria to facilitate resolution of the Darfur crisis.

Though much of this history occurred before Jonathan came to power, it is important to remember Nigeria's often overlooked role in bringing stability to the region and on the continent. Goodluck Jonathan's policies of engagement have thus been a mark of continuity rather than a radical new direction.

During the Presidency of Olusegun Obasanjo, who was regarded as much as a global statesman as a Nigerian politician, one analyst described his ministers as "nothing more than the President's companions on foreign trips", adding: "Obasanjo micromanaged Nigeria's foreign affairs the same way he micromanaged the energy sector." Jonathan, however, has a very different management style, though no less effective. "In Nigeria a leader must be in charge of everything, and if you delegate well then that is a sign of weakness," observes Antony Goldman. "Then that must mean that you are not interested or are not in control of things. I think it is a pity, because it is only when you give people the responsibility and they live up to that that you can begin to strengthen institutions properly. In foreign affairs Jonathan has got some very good people who have done some good things, in Africa and in the world more broadly."

The first flashpoint that occurred just as the transition was happening in Abuja was in November 2010 when Cote d'Ivoire unravelled following the presidential election contested by the incumbent Laurent Gbagbo and the man who was to be declared the winner Alassane Ouattara. When Gbagbo refused to accept the result, Nigeria mounted a diplomatic campaign backed by the US, the United Nations and European powers, underpinned by the threat of financial sanctions and military action if Gbagbo failed to relinquish power. It was to no avail and the then Nigerian Foreign Minister Odein Ajumogobia was forced to announce that a bloc of Western African countries was seeking UN support for military intervention to end the dispute. Ajumogobia expressed concern that, if there is no action against Gbagbo, it would set a bad example in advance of a rash of elections that were due to take place over the coming eighteen months in Africa.

"It is clear that Gbagbo is determined to defy and treat the entire international community with absolute disdain... he cannot, he must not be allowed to prevail," Ajumogobia wrote in a strongly-worded piece for Nigeria's ThisDay newspaper. "The political crisis in Cote d'Ivoire is likely to disrupt the trend towards democracy in the sub region and create a dangerous precedent for a continent in which 20 presidential elections are to hold within the next 18 months. Consequently, the impunity of Gbagbo must be regarded as a challenge to the entire international community. Gbagbo must be made to understand that there is a very real prospect of overwhelming military capability bearing down on him and his cohorts."

Gbagbo responded to the international calls for him to stand down in typically bellicose fashion. His army, backed by Liberian mercenaries, began attacking ethnic northerners in the capital Abidjan. The tide soon turned, however, and forces loyal to Ouattara took control in April 2011. Gbagbo himself was arrested by UN forces and transferred to the ICC in The Hague that November, where he still languishes awaiting trial.

No sooner was the Cote d'Ivoire situation resolved than the Libyan crisis came to a head. As we have seen, Nigeria – under Jonathan – once again took a leading role. Before the question of recognition for the NTC came up, however, there had already been signs that the AU was taking an over-cautious line. It was not until March, 2011, that it finally issued a statement expressing "deep concern" over the violence in Libya. Three African countries sitting on the United Nations Security Council – Nigeria, South Africa and Gabon – supported the council's resolution on authorising the no-fly zone over Libya and "all necessary measures" to protect civilians. Five other countries abstained, namely Russia, China, Brazil, Germany and India. The same countries endorsed resolution 1970 imposing comprehensive sanctions on the Libyan leader and his henchmen as well as referring the crimes committed by his regime to the International Criminal Court (ICC), an organization routinely criticized by the AU.

While it supported the enforcement of a no-fly zone, South Africa objected to NATO's military intervention in Libya and so when Nigeria recognised the NTC it came as a surprise to many. Gambia had been the first African nation to take this position and it had been followed by Senegal but both countries were relative minnows. It was Nigeria's decision that really mattered.

Abuja reasserted its position as a rival to South Africa as the region's leading powerbroker in January 2013 when West African nations agreed to send some 3,000 troops to help Mali wrest back control of its northern half, which had been seized by Al-Qaeda-linked fighters. Again, the largest number of troops came from Nigeria, which agreed to send over 700 soldiers. The remaining troops came from the other nations in the ECOWAS bloc.

A large number of Nigerians strongly opposed the deployment of their troops to Mali for combat duties. Many viewed Mali's internal problems in much the same way Britain's prime minister Neville Chamberlain saw Nazi Germany's harassment of Czechoslovakia in 1938: "a quarrel in a faraway country between people of whom we know nothing". Why should Nigerian soldiers be sent "somewhere in the Sahara" to fight and, in some cases, die? Liberia and Sierra Leone shared a border and were neighbours. But Mali?

Many also complained that President Jonathan had no business playing the regional Sergeant-Major when he seemed incapable of subduing Boko Haram at home. At the time, it was killing people almost at will all over northern Nigeria. But Jonathan argued that it was precisely because of the havoc caused by Boko Haram that Nigeria could not just sit and watch Mali go under. Al-Qaeda and other jihadists were believed to have chosen northern Mali as the base for spreading their campaign across West Africa, and their most prized target was Nigeria.

"We believe that if we stabilise northern Mali, not just Nigeria but other countries that are facing threats will be stabilised," said Jonathan. "The terrorists have no boundaries. They don't respect international boundaries… If we do not contain the problem of Mali, definitely it will affect other African countries and that is why Nigeria had to move fast. If the crisis is not properly checked, it has the potentials of increasing investment risks in the African continent. If the region was made stable, we would not have had those crises in Libya and Mali would have been better than what it is now. One fundamental problem in Mali is the issue of governance and religious extremism. The terrorist aspect and issue of hostage taking for the purposes of ransom and drug traffickers happened because of the crisis in Libya and of course the terrorists will always want to instigate crisis because they make money out of it."

The Chief of Army Staff, Lieutenant General Azubuike Ihejirika, echoed this sentiment, saying that Mali-trained terrorists had entered the country: "We are aware that most of the terrorists in this country today were trained in Mali. We are also aware that, as we speak, there was still an influx of some chaps trained in Mali into the country." He added: "Nigeria will not only be supporting the resolution of the international community, but also enhancing its own security and that of its immediate neighbours by undertaking this operation. What we are going into could be described as peace enforcement; that is to bring peace with the use of force. And as to whether the operation will be conventional or insurgent, the troops should have a mixture of both because of the characters of the rebels."

According to the then Foreign Affairs Minister, Olugbenga Ashiru, Nigeria was the ultimate target of the terrorists operating in northern Mali. "The deployment of Nigerian troops to Mali was in the best interest of Nigeria," he said, arguing the government should do everything possible to ensure that the terrorists did not achieve their aim. "The events in Mali, if we don't quickly stop it, will have effect on the whole of West Africa and Nigeria is the prime target," he said. "So, we need to act quickly, forcefully, in Mali to stop them, to contain them, to destroy their capability to be able to launch any counter offensive within the sub-region."[2]

Nigeria was not going at it alone, of course. France was leading the intervention and troops from Burkina Faso and Niger, which were also in danger of attack, joined Nigeria in the Malian desert.

Nigeria remains the military powerhouse and the regional superpower in West Africa, if not the continent as a whole, to this day. With 170 million people, Nigeria is not only Africa's most populous country but one with a bigger population than all the other 14 ECOWAS member states put together. It is also the continent's largest producer of oil. This confers on it obligations as well as privileges. Nigeria finances two thirds of the ECOWAS budget and is Africa's second-highest troop-contributing country for UN peacekeeping missions worldwide. Thanks to the fact that its security services are on constant alert due to years of violent conflict with separatists in the Niger Delta and the terrorists of Boko Haram in the north it can also boast they are among the most battle-hardened soldiers around.

The government believes that "a threat to peace anywhere in Africa is a threat to peace everywhere on the continent." After all, its role in peacekeeping, conflict prevention and resolution is not limited to the West African sub-region. It also contributed to the end of apartheid in South Africa, and has been involved in conflict resolution as far afield as Chad, Burundi, the Democratic Republic of the Congo, Zimbabwe, and Ethiopia–Eritrea, as well as Liberia, Sierra Leone, Darfur, Cote d'Ivoire, Libya and Mali. It has been estimated that Nigeria has so far spent over $12 billion on its various peacekeeping campaigns. And the price has been paid in blood as well as treasure. A large number of men and women of the Nigerian Armed Forces have made the supreme sacrifice in the cause of peace in the region.

"That is an area that as an administration they get all too little credit for," argues the analyst Anthony Goldman. "There was a decade of turmoil in Cote d'Ivoire, and Nigeria was the only country that was going to back French intervention in 2010. They were going to do it despite what South Africa thought, despite what the AU said, and they were right, and I think it has been shown that they were right with the progress that Ivory Coast has made since then. They backed intervention in Libya, they backed intervention in Mali. The rest of the world matters quite a lot to Nigeria and I think they have shown that they can take difficult decisions, and sometimes at the risk of falling out with allies. They haven't always followed the West's line, its Nigeria's line. And if that coincides with France, the US or the UK well then Nigeria backs it. With Kenyatta and the criminal court they followed their own independent line there as well. In fact I think Nigeria has got quite a good record of leadership on politics and security in the region. And I am not sure Nigeria always gets the credit for that."

Jonathan has made the promotion of peace and security in Africa one of his primary foreign policy objectives based on a conviction that economic development and regional integration cannot be superimposed on an unstable region. Nor can Africa meet the challenges of poverty reduction and the elimination of diseases, unless there is peace and security on the continent.

Meanwhile the disposition of powers in the great game has changed and Nigeria has developed a new-found self confidence. "We have woken up from sleep, we are big boys, we know what we want," one former foreign minister said in an interview with the Financial Times. "Standards that are not acceptable in your own countries – in Britain, or Holland or America – will not be acceptable here." Nigeria believes it can now demand more of its partners, a more reciprocal relationship – or "adult" relationship.

Today China, the US and a number of other nations are trying to broaden and deepen their influence in what will be Africa's largest market in decades to come. The British have the longest pedigree in the country, but there has been a long-standing relationship with the US and other European powers as well. Since independence, successive Nigerian governments adopted a broadly pro-Western stance and the country became an important partner for the US. Jonathan's approach of non-partisanship has meant that China, Brazil, Turkey, South Korea and Russia have all increased their engagement, but not as Cold War rivals.

Still, the relationship with the US can be prickly. For long periods the Nigerians felt their friendship was undervalued, and US-Nigerian relations have wavered throughout the decades. From the start America treated Africa as a theatre in which the power politics of the Cold War had to be played out. It focused too narrowly on merely trying to block Soviet expansion in the continent. When it came to Nigeria, its diplomacy was driven by broad doctrines rather than detailed assessments of the country and a willingness to be flexible. In his book, "Nigeria, Africa, And The United States: From Kennedy To Reagan," Robert B. Shepard traces US-Nigerian relations over six American administrations. Shepard argues that US policy toward Nigeria has never had much to do with what was going on there or in Africa as a whole. Instead, American policy makers saw what they wanted to see and proceeded accordingly. "Policy was driven by doctrine, not facts," Shepard wrote. [1]

The US today considers Nigeria in many respects its most important partner in Africa, says Jonny Carson, former US Assistant Secretary of State for Africa. This despite the fact that the US, once the largest customer for Nigerian oil, buys only a fraction of what it used to, as it has been displaced by the light oil from the shale of North Dakota. Nigerian oil production is still crucial for the stability of global energy markets. Jennifer Cooke, Director of the Africa Programme at the Center for Strategic and International Studies, says the US sees Nigeria as the largest country in Africa, as a country that is hugely significant both as a regional peace keeper and as a country that is facing its own security challenges. "The US sees Nigeria's successes as having potentially catalytic consequences for Africa, and it sees its failings as having consequences for Africa way beyond Nigeria."

Cooke says it's a complicated and sometimes frustrating relationship, but "there is a basic affinity between the two countries in terms of their outlook on regional and global affairs that other big partnerships on the continent, such as Angola and South Africa, lack. It's a complicated relationship because Nigeria is a complicated place and the US expects a lot of Nigeria because it's a basically good relationship."

China, on the other hand, is a relative newcomer and its initial 'oil-for-infrastructure' model for engagement with Nigeria has been a failure. Under this arrangement, Nigeria gave oil blocks to Chinese energy companies in return for the completion of infrastructure projects built by Chinese companies and financed by Chinese banks. This was the model adopted by former President Obasanjo and Nigeria–China relations intensified during his second term, from 2003 to 2007, when President Hu Jintao and Prime Minister Wen Jiabao of China both visited Nigeria and Obasanjo twice went to Beijing. The intergovernmental Nigeria–China Investment

Forum was founded in 2006 and Obasanjo used his position as his own Minister of Petroleum to award several major oil blocks to Chinese companies in return for significant infrastructure-building commitments from China. By this stage, the signs were that both Nigeria and China had developed relatively coherent policies towards each other, both seemingly firmly rooted in economic interests. However, few of the infrastructure projects were completed and none of the blocks that China was awarded have been developed.

The only active way Chinese energy companies have gained access to the Nigeria's oil resources is by buying stakes in established western companies, such as when Sinopec bought Addax. Though there are now large numbers of Chinese living and working in the country – from factory managers to traders – and cheap Chinese goods are on sale throughout the country, Chinese investment in Nigeria comes nowhere near to challenging that of the established US and the European powers.

At the end of the day, Jonathan has based his diplomacy on the strength of the Nigerian economy, and relations with the big powers are based on the commercial attractiveness of investment in the country. This, coupled with a non-partisan approach, has ensured that countries as diverse as Brazil, Turkey, Ukraine, South Africa, South Korea, and India have all invested in Nigeria during the last five years.

Chapter Nine

JIHAD INC – THE HIDDEN AGENDA BEHIND BOKO HARAM

When commanders of the Islamist sect Boko Haram wrote to President Goodluck Jonathan in September 2014 seeking a deal to end Africa's bloodiest terrorist conflict, the man entrusted to lead the talks was Ambassador Hassan Tukur, his Principal Private Secretary. Tukur was a low-key and thoughtful former diplomat and long-time advisor to Nigerian heads of state. He was the ultimate insider and behind the scenes fixer. Not only had he become the most influential Muslim in the Presidential Villa, he was a close friend of the President. It was this unlikely partnership of a northerner and a southerner, a devout Muslim and a devout Christian, in a country increasingly divided between north and south that was to drive the push for a deal to end the violence and secure the release of the Chibok girls and hundreds of other hostages.

Tukur described his friendship with Jonathan as transcending the usual boundaries that separate Nigerians. "Jonathan is not a stereotypical Nigerian where you have to be from the same state or region to be friends," explained Tukur in an interview with the authors, adding that he thought that one of the President's strongest qualities is his humility. "He doesn't care where you come from. When we met, he was Deputy Governor of Bayelsa and I was just a civil servant, he was from the South and I was from the North but he wanted to be my friend. He cares more about the qualities of who you are."

The President was aware of one special quality that would help Tukur weave his way through the treacherous political underworld of West Africa: as a consummate diplomat he would have to accommodate the governments and security forces of Chad and Cameroon, as well as Northern Nigeria's ethnic, religious and ideological forces and factions, not to mention securing the support of the Nigerian military. And that is even before he even sat down to talk to the notoriously fractious Boko Haram leadership with its multiple agendas, sponsors and connections with international terrorism.

When Tukur spoke to the representatives of Boko Haram, the menace of violent terrorism in the form of suicide bombings, kidnappings and random mass killings had loomed over Nigeria for almost five years. Since 2009, Boko Haram had resorted to extreme levels of brutality and atrocity. But in 2014, after a lull during the previous year, there was a dramatic increase in explosions, killings, rapes and abductions.

Between January and August 2014, Boko Haram was responsible for the deaths of more than 4,000 people. The insurgents became more violent and strategic – targeting and killing civilians in over 70 towns and villages in the rural north-east as they spread terror. "Boko Haram is effectively waging war on the people of north eastern Nigeria at a staggering human cost," said Corinne Dufka, West Africa director at Human Rights Watch.

What made the world wake up to this terror was the kidnapping of 276 young girls from a school in Chibok just before midnight on April 14, 2014. It was not Boko Haram's first attack on schools in the north-east, and would not be the last. Two months earlier they locked the doors to a boys' dormitory at the State College of Buni Yadi, a secondary school near Damaturu, Yobe State, and set the building on fire, killing 59 pupils by burning them alive.

The scale of the Chibok abduction was unprecedented. Sitting in her office in the Office of the National Security Adviser, Fatima Akilu, the Director of Behavioural Analysis and Strategic Communication, recalled her thoughts at the moment she heard about Chibok:

"There are many things that made Chibok different and distinctive. The sheer audacity of kidnapping so many girls at once. The idea that these girls were sitting their exams preparing for their next stage in life. After that they would have continued on with university. Also the fact that they were taken alive, so there was hope and that was exploited by many people, for better or worse. These girls were taken in the backdrop of the massacre at the College of Buni Yadi, and I remember feeling pure horror and thinking that there must soon come a demand, a ransom, because there must be a reason why they would take such a large number. There were rumours of a ransom. We heard about it from our people on the ground in Maiduguri. But no one ever stepped forward.

"I think people underestimate how Boko Haram operate. They arrive in large convoys. They are all dressed in military fatigues, their cars are painted in military colours. When they attacked Chibok that night they pretended they were the military. They had detonated some explosives outside of the town, close enough for the girls and their teachers to hear those bombs go off, so there was some commotion. Then they drove up to the school, looking like the military, and claiming to be the army. They told the girls that they were there to save them from Boko Haram who was attacking the school. There was nothing indicating that they were lying. They looked exactly like the military, and the girls had heard the bombs go off. That's why they went with them voluntarily. They thought they were going to safety. That was why they were able to round them up so quickly and kidnap so many. The girls that escaped later told us that they didn't realise it wasn't the military until they had been driven into the forest. There, at one point, the car broke down and they managed to escape."

The Chibok kidnapping had all the hallmarks of a co-ordinated and pre-meditated operation. Earlier that day, almost 800 kilometres away, an explosion at a bus station packed with morning commuters at Nyanya, on the southern outskirts of Abuja, killed at least 88 people and injured another 125. Because of its proximity to the capital, this incident attracted a lot of media attention, even though it would not make it into the top five on a list of Boko Haram's deadliest attacks of 2014. The bombing had the effect of distracting the military authorities and so when the reports of the Chibok kidnapping came in they were simply buried by the avalanche of security, military and civil defence reports on the Abuja atrocity.

National security officials believed that it was not a coincidence that the bus station bombing in Nyanya occurred just hours before the kidnapping of the Chibok girls in order to stretch the resources of military and security officials. Their focus was now whether the new sophisticated approach indicated that Boko Haram was being manipulated by other Jihadi elements.

The explosion at the bus station was not an isolated act of terror. It was a declaration of war. Soon afterwards a man claiming to be "Shekau" described the bombing as a "tiny incident", and warned of many more to come. In a video he stared into the camera and taunted President Jonathan: "You are just too small for us. We are in your city, but you don't know where we are".

True to his word, these were not isolated incidents. Three weeks later, Boko Haram fighters murdered 336 people in the towns of Gamboru and Ngala during an attack in which they used two armoured personnel carriers they had stolen from the Nigerian military.

The villages were burned to the ground. A recurrent and familiar tactic was emerging: Boko Haram "soldiers", dressed in military fatigue, would deceive their victims into a false sense of security and then moments later, when they are all rounded up, cut their throats and then film the grisly episode. "It is not about killing you quickly, it is about you suffering", said Akilu. "Even if they have plenty of bullets, they still prefer to cut your throat. That is their modus operandi. They have gone so far, now it is very difficult to go back and modify their methods. If you were Shekau and responsible for the deaths of thousands of people, it is easier for you to hang onto your beliefs, because the alternative of confronting what you have done is just too awful. How can you live with yourself if you accept what you have done? How do you answer to God, in whose name you say you have committed these atrocities? So in a perverse kind of way it is easier to continue"

On 20 May 2014, an explosion that killed more than 100 people in the town of Jos signalled a frightening new dimension to the indiscriminate carnage by the insurgents. The Boko Haram insurgency so far had various agendas: the absence of a clear leadership or political program has made it hard to discern exactly what they want. But there is little doubt about the message of the Jos bombings: it was an attempt to break open an old wound in a part of the country where ethnic and religious tensions have often resulted in sectarian violence.

Nigeria is the world's largest experiment of peaceful coexistence between Islam and Christianity. The country is home to approximately 170 million people, equally divided between Muslims and Christians. While the North is predominantly Muslim and the South is predominantly Christian, people of both faiths live side-by-side tolerating one another throughout the country. However, friction has erupted into sectarian bloodletting between Christian and Muslim communities in Plateau state, driven by conflicts over land between largely Christian indigenes and Muslim Fulani herders.

The move to extend the campaign into the state capital of Plateau, in Nigeria's Middle Belt, with the potential to catapult the insurgency into a Christian versus Muslim and ethnic dimension showed a tactical imagination beyond the capacity of the thugs who had thus far paraded themselves on video as "Boko Haram". The bomb in Jos was expertly coordinated and detonated while the military and security apparatus was pre-occupied with searching for the Chibok girls in the North East and responding to the Abuja and Kano bombings.

Meanwhile, intense international concern at the Chibok kidnappings drew a huge contingent of foreign correspondents to Nigeria and the eyes of the world were on every development. The timing worked for the insurgents: on 7 May 2014 the world's media gathered in Abuja for the World Economic Forum to cover the story of Africa's rise, the showcase of which was Nigeria's emergence as the continent's largest economy. But instead all the dispatches were about the missing girls. Any accomplishments of the Jonathan administration were completely overshadowed by its perceived inability to contain the insurgency. It had been a devastating propaganda coup against the government.

This was encouragement to the bloody and relentless onslaught that continued. Boko Haram fired at people gathered in busy markets, places of worship and residential neighbourhoods. In June 2014, they again used their familiar tactic of impersonating military personnel to round up hundreds of civilians in three villages in Gwoza, Borno State, and promptly opened fire, leaving 110 people dead. "This is not about Islam or Christianity", said one intelligence official. "We are long past that stage. They are using religion as their cover, because this has nothing to do with religion. This is purely about creating an ungovernable chaos"

These mass murders were on an unprecedented scale even by international terrorist standards and it was clear that they could no longer be justified on the basis of religion. "They have many motivations, but it has nothing to do with Islam", said Akilu. "When they first started under Yusuf, I think they acted within the confines of their own understanding of Islam. That is no longer the case. When I read Qumea I understood that he was actually a reformer. Therein lies the paradox: today they preach and want to revert to a society of the 16th century, but these are the very ideas and society that Qumea fought against. It is clear that they do not have a comprehensive understanding of the text that they themselves are quoting from.

"What happened under Shekau is so far away from religion. I think he always liked the idea of himself as the 'soldier', the 'military commander', but he is not charismatic enough to hold a group based on his leadership qualities and so he ruled by fear and dressed in military fatigue. He fancied himself as this big figure and the media has given him this huge platform. Now they are responding to this new international audience. We have been looking at the media coverage and whenever the coverage increased their activity spiked, so it was clear that they responded to their newfound stardom. They make sure to always keep themselves in the news. And so I do think this has contributed to the way the movement has moved in recent times."

Boko Haram, it was clear, was fighting an increasingly sophisticated war of armed propaganda in which social media was used to project its message and spread fear. Much of the media has been its unwitting ally, according to the American analyst Jacob Zenn: "The media must be aware that it can be a tool for publicizing the agendas of terrorists groups, even unknowingly. The international media must strengthen internal due diligence and evaluate the impact of reporting Islamic extremist propaganda."

And yet it would be wrong to downplay the religious origins of Boko Haram. Their real name is the Jama'atu Ahlul Sunnah Lih Da'awa wal Jihad (JAS) but it became widely known as Boko Haram, which in Hausa means "western education is sinful". However, the literal translation distorts its origin. Boko Haram began as opposition to what was regarded as the corrupt behaviour of the elite in the North of the country, who in their thinking had become estranged from true Islam, and sought a purification of Islam in Nigeria. The sect never opposed education. Instead their "hostility" to western schooling emanated from the sons and daughters of the Hausa/Fulani elite being sent to expensive schools and colleges in the UK and USA.

Boko Haram springs from the Sunni Izala movement (also known as the Society of Removal of Innovation and Re-Establishment of the Sunni). The term Izala is a form of Islamic fundamentalism, related to Salafism, which is widespread in Saudi Arabia and produced extremist splinter groups in many parts of the world. The Izala Sunnis regard many Muslim regimes as corrupt and seek a return to the "true" practice of Islam.

Izala, initially at least, did not advocate the violent overthrow of the government to create an Islamic state – that was a later interpretation. Instead, they sought the return of all Muslims to the "true practice" of Islam consistent with teachings found in the Qu'ran and the practices of the Prophet Muhammad.

The founder of Izala was Sheikh Ababubakar Gumi (1922-1992), an Islamic scholar and Grand Khadi of the Northern Region of Nigeria (1962–1967). His protégé was Mohammed Yusuf, a member of the Jakusku tribe in Yobe State, who became a senior figure in the JAS. Yusuf had studied the Quran with his father and became a devoted Izala member in the tradition of Sheikh Gumi. He later married a daughter of the local leader Alhaji Baa Fugu Mohammed, on whose land in Maiduguri a mosque was built where Yusuf then taught the Boko Haram ideology.

In the early years of Boko Haram, Sheikh Ja`afar Mahmoud Adam, a Kano-based cleric, was the elder who led the sect and preached at the Indimi mosque in Maiduguri. But he criticised the young Yusuf for teaching excessive and extremist interpretations of Islam. Yusuf promised to repent, but in a power grab promptly arranged for the older man to be killed as he was leading morning prayers at the Dorayi Juma'at Mosque.

Violence was never far from the surface and yet Boko Haram was brought close to the center of power when they worked on behalf of the Governor of Borno state, Ali Modu Sheriff, during the 2003 and 2007 elections. However, they fell out with the authorities, and in July 2009, during the

Presidency of Alhaji Yar' Adua, Boko Haram members were involved in a shootout with police after they were stopped in Maiduguri for not wearing helmets while driving motorbikes, which was against the law (their defence was that they could not fit the helmets over their turbans).

The deaths of Boko Haram members led to attacks on police headquarters and government buildings. Pitched battles followed and the military and police killed Boko Haram members over a four-day period and arrested hundreds more. Some of those arrested remained in prison for prolonged periods without charge. This included Yusuf who later died in police custody. As a result its activists began to embrace terrorism in earnest.

Presidential advisor Hassan Tukur was with Jonathan when the violence erupted in 2009. "When Yusuf was killed, I was with Jonathan. He was then the Vice President, and we saw it all on TV. I remember he said that 'this is not acceptable, that cannot happen. A police officer cannot take the law into his own hands.' The President doesn't accept this lawlessness. That is why he feels so strongly that there must be this rule of law."

The death of Yusuf in July 2009 was a pivotal event for the Yusufiya faction and a watershed for Boko Haram. His demise and the subsequent reprisal attacks in Maiduguri and surrounding areas did much to radicalize elements in the group and increase Boko Haram's membership. Prior to this event, Yusuf's following only amounted to perhaps 1,000 guerrillas or passive sympathizers with largely localized aims. Today that number is closer to 10,000.

In July 2010, Abubakar bin Muhammed Shekau, Yusuf's former second-in-command who led Boko Haram's military wing, emerged from hiding to publicly claim leadership of the group. Over time, the Boko Haram split into three principal groups. Firstly, the Yusufiya – a group of Yusuf loyalists loosely led by Shekau who are known as "core" or "radical" Boko Haram. Secondly, a network of opportunists who exploited the climate of fear, confusion and insecurity in parts of the Northeast to engage in criminal acts such as bank robberies and kidnappings. And, finally, there was a group that relied on local and regional supporters for money, arms and ammunition.

When Goodluck Jonathan became President in 2010, Boko Haram had been active for some time. By then, they had state-level commanders in many Nigerian states, most of them organized under Shekau. In some frontline states, such as Borno, there was a commander for each local government area, and the overall command structure resembled a professional military command hierarchy.

The radicalization of Shekau and core Boko Haram leaders like third-in-command Mamman Nur led them to identify and sympathize more closely with Al-Qaeda. Shekau and other commanders moved underground and began to refocus the group's ideology – or at least its rhetoric – more towards global jihad and planning suicide bombings. Following the killing of Osama bin Laden, Shekau adopted the nom de guerre "al Zawahiri," after Al-Qaeda second-in-command Dr. Ayman al'Zawahiri.

Today Al-Qaeda is actively backing Boko Haram by

training their operatives in nearby Mali and has a network of associated Islamist groups spanning Chad, Cameroon, Niger, Sudan and northern Mali. The group has received support in the form of weaponry from Mokthar Belmokthar, an Algerian Jihadist who operates in Algeria, Mali and Niger under the auspices of his group, Al-Qaeda Islamic Maghreb (AQIM), which has also exchanged operatives with Boko Haram. Belmokthar has despatched manpower into northern Nigeria in exchange for shipments of Boko Haram operatives to support his actions in northern Mali.

Abdelhamid Amli, another known AQIM facilitator operating mainly in southern Algeria and Niger, was tasked with recruiting youth from poor Hausa neighbourhoods in northern Nigeria in 2000. Three years later, an unknown number of recruits reportedly travelled through Sudan and Syria to Iraq, to fight against the US-led occupation.

One notable Boko Haram terrorist was Khalid al-Barnawi from Borno state, who trained with AQIM in Algeria in the mid-2000s before returning to kidnap foreigners in Niger and Nigeria. Al-Barnawi is also on the list of three Nigerians whom the United States designated as "global terrorists" in June 2012. Nigeria later declared the same three persons "Most Wanted" for participating in Boko Haram's "Shura Council". A few Boko Haram commanders have ties to other Middle Eastern and African terrorist groups. For example, Mamman Nur who claims to have trained with Somalia's al-Shabaab, an Al-Qaeda affiliate.

Many of Boko Haram's weapons are obtained from past and ongoing conflicts in Algeria, Libya and Sudan. These arms have been smuggled into Nigeria by fighters and arms brokers from these countries as well as from Chad. In the case of Mali, guns have come into Nigeria in exchange for Boko Haram providing operatives to support action against French and Nigerian troops in northern Mali.

In late 2010, as the terrorist attacks reached a new and more lethal phase, some Nigerian politicians appeared to support Boko Haram, at least in rhetoric, and a few even supplied them with financing and operational support. As the sect grew in influence and became more militant, they recruited unemployed young men who were co-opted as private armies for political campaigns. Their motivation was brazenly political: to portray President Jonathan as unable to contain the violence in the North, and therefore not fit to govern. There were recurrent allegations that supporters of Boko Haram included top Northern politicians hostile to the President including members of the opposition party.

On October 4, 2010, Jonathan installed Andrew Azazi as the new National Security Adviser. A Christian southerner from the same state as the President, he was vastly experienced and had been Chief of Defence Staff under former President Obasanjo. Jonathan thought Azazi was the right man for the job. However, Azazi, who later died in a helicopter crash in 2012, never favoured negotiations with Boko Haram and instead focused solely on a military solution. "We will defeat the insurgents by military force", he said. "This deal will never stick".

But Jonathan remained determined to stop the bloodshed and open to the possibility of a settlement. As Vice-President, he had overseen an agreement with militants in the Niger Delta. That was a conflict he understood. He was from the Niger Delta and could identify with their struggle. But Boko Haram leaders were from the north and this presented a disadvantage for the President who had never lived in that region. And so he relied on Northerners to guide him, just like Yar' Adua had relied on him to bring peace to the Niger Delta.

After the election in 2011, Boko Haram escalated its indiscriminate attacks and the crisis worsened. The stated aim of the new attacks was crudely political: to destabilize the country. That summer also marked their first use of targeted suicide bombings. On August 26, 2011, a suicide bomber drove a vehicle containing an improvised explosive device into the United Nations headquarters in Abuja, killing 23 people and injuring more than 80 others. Boko Haram claimed responsibility for the atrocity, one of the deadliest in the history of the United Nations. While this attack occurred inside Nigerian borders, it was the first time Boko Haram had targeted an international, non-Nigerian entity.

The abduction of a French family in Cameroon in 2013, since attributed to Ansaru, an offshoot of Boko Haram, was a sign that the group had strengthened its strategic ties with Al-Qaeda Islamic Maghreb (AQIM). Nigerian Intelligence officials believed that local mercenaries kidnapped the French family and then sold them to the terrorists. This mirrored AQIM's established practice of kidnapping people outside its core operating areas and then transporting them to a safe haven.

In response to the impasse and the failure of the military to stop Boko Haram activities, in 2012 President Jonathan chose a Northerner, retired Colonel Sambo Dasuki, as his new National Security Advisor. It was believed that he would have a better understanding of the regional backdrop to the conflict. Dasuki is part of the core Northern elite, and a member of the Sokoto royal family. He had been the aide-de-camp to former military heads of state and a power broker to retired General Ibrahim Babangida. He had family ties with one of his predecessors Aliyu Mohammed Gusau, who has served multiple times as the national security advisor and is now Minister of Defence. This appeared to be a smart choice: the security crisis in the North was now in the hands of Northerners.

But the situation continued to deteriorate. Despite an increase in the military budget and more soldiers, Boko Haram continued to terrorise the nation. The Nigerian people were increasingly impatient: Jonathan was criticised for being ineffective and not acting enough and the military for over-reacting. Meanwhile Dasuki was quietly implementing a new strategy to defeat Boko Haram that did not rely solely on a military solution.

The pace of attacks intensified in May 2013. President Jonathan responded by declaring a six month-long state of emergency in the north-eastern states of Borno, Adamawa, and Yobe and ordered extra troops to restore order. The announcement represented Nigeria's version of the US surge in Afghanistan. Critics argued that the military's response to Boko Haram's trail of destruction was indiscriminate, disproportionate and counter-productive. Human Rights Watch chronicled a military raid on Baga in April 2013 that left 2,000 burned homes and 183 dead bodies. The Nigerian military however denied the figures and blamed the atrocities on the insurgents. They said that the Human Rights Watch figure of 2,000 far exceeded the total number of houses in the town. This raid was skillfully exploited by a section of the political opposition who lost no opportunity to tarnish the image of the military in order to undermine the government's efforts to defeat Boko Haram.

In the Autumn of 2013, President Jonathan, after widespread calls for dialogue by prominent northern elders, established a 26-member committee, headed by Special Duties Minister Kabiru Tanimu Turaki, to discuss disarmament and an amnesty for some Boko Haram members. This was the first time such an approach was formally and officially acknowledged by the government. Boko Haram members were given a 60-day window within which to disarm.

By now, Boko Haram fighters were operating with apparent impunity from towns like Kungarawa on the Chad border and Gambaru on the Cameroon border. According to an intelligence source the insurgents were "diving back and forth across the border" into Nigeria causing mayhem. Collaboration was needed with the governments of Niger, Chad, Cameroon and Sudan.

In May 2013, Jonathan agreed and after weeks of delicate and sensitive negotiations between the factions, 26 representatives of the Boko Haram leadership met in Abuja to engage in talks with government officials from Nigeria, Niger, Chad, Cameroon and Sudan.

Shekau, the head of Boko Haram, agreed that the governing Shura Council should proceed with the dialogue. They chose their delegates who were dispatched to Abuja for meetings with the government. But Shekau's envoy then stipulated preconditions for the talks. A key demand was the release of women and children taken into custody as a result of the military sweep through northern villages and towns.

"Shekau is willing to enter a peace accord on the terms set out by Mr. President", stated the envoy. "As a step of good faith, the government must release women and children. As soon as the women and children are released and arrests ceased, Shekau will order a ceasefire and personally attend talks."

The President was shocked when he was informed about this request, mainly because he did not know women and children were being held in detention, according to one government insider. "The military and intelligence chiefs had not revealed any such information to Jonathan. Officially it was as if they did not exist," the source said. Jonathan immediately authorised their release. As this included the wife of Shekau there was a surge of goodwill from both sides.

This sense of progress was confirmed on 25 May 2013, when Sheik Ahmed Gumi, the son of the Izala founder and a major figure in Boko Haram, publicly called on "all those killing people, including Boko Haram members, must stop. They are destroying themselves, and they can never succeed". The Sheikh added that Boko Haram members "cannot kill someone and expect peace; they will not live to enjoy the killings they did. Nigerians must live in peace; everyone needs good health, shelter, education and a better future for their children. Leaders should not be biased at all level; they should serve all Muslims, Christians, and in fact they should serve the whole country."

There was cautious optimism around the talks. But then in June 2013, came surprising news: Shekau, the head of Boko Haram, had allegedly been shot dead. Commanders of the Shura Council informed the stunned committee and claimed that Shekau had apparently been killed by one of his own acolytes. According to senior commanders close to Shekau, it appeared that Shekau was no longer interested in the negotiations and was given a stark choice: he could join the peace dialogue with the Nigerian Government, form his own sect or face execution. It appears that he chose death. Senior Boko Haram commanders, including Shekau's Chief of Security, Abdullahi Hassan, confirmed that Shekau was then shot and buried.

Two weeks later a man calling himself Shekau and looking several years younger suddenly popped up on youtube. "It was clear to everyone that he was an imposter, and several Shura Council members confirmed it", said the intelligence source. "But his name was a lucrative franchise and without Shekau the credibility and viability of Boko Haram was doubtful."

According to Hassan Tukur, the president's envoy, it no longer matters whether Shekau is alive or dead. "Twice there were claims he was dead, but then he comes back with another video", he told the authors"But the person who appears on the youtube videos is not always the same. Shekau is a phenomina and a spokesperson for the group. He could have died years ago, and he could still be alive. Anybody can take his name. At one point we had sources who spoke of an Imam called Bashir, who portrayed himself as Shekau. This Imam was killed in the battle of Konduga. But really it is irrelevant if Shekau is dead or alive. It is the Shura Council who ultimately governs Boko Haram. It is the Shura Council you must negotiate with, they are the ones who take the decisions and it have always been so, not the man who at any one moment calls himself Shekau on a youtube video."

The peace process limped on but eventually broke down in August 2013 and any prospect of a peace deal with Boko Haram appeared to have been curtailed. Those within government opposed to negotiation felt vindicated and the kidnappings and bombings continued. On 14 November, 2013, Boko Haram was designated as a Foreign Terrorist Organization by the United States and their most extreme operatives were now in the ascendency.

The struggle was no longer simply about the purification of Islam that had been preached by its founder Mohammed Yusuf. Instead, a far more virulent element had emerged, secretly funded by powerful sponsors within Nigeria with the aim of creating chaos and discrediting the administration. It was a thinly disguised attempt at a coup d'etat.

The biggest problem was that bordering countries were not sharing sufficient intelligence on the insurgents with the Nigerian security agencies because of fears that the supporters of Boko Haram would take revenge by launching terrorist raids in their own territory. "There was a breakdown in trust with Cameroon, Niger and Chad", said one security adviser. "In the past prior intelligence from border countries was a crucial factor in countering terrorist acts. But now convoys of 40 to 60 Boko Haram vehicles with armed personnel carriers and 100 heavily armed men were left free to massacre villagers, kidnap boys and rape girls."

The President now took several steps in an attempt to make a critical difference. The first was a step up the military campaign against the insurgency, while leaving the door open for negotiations, and the second was to create a regional security alliance to combat the sect. A summit in Paris on May 17, 2014, hosted by French President Francois Hollande, brought the neighbouring nations of Nigeria, Benin, Cameroon, Niger and Chad and the Western powers together to agree on a plan to seal the borders, share intelligence and co-ordinate military responses. The countries also agreed to dispatch a joint crack force of 700 soldiers to target Boko Haram.

Following the rapid success of another terror group, – Islamic State (ISIS) – in gaining territories in Iraq and Syria, Boko Haram gradually changed its tactics in Nigeria by focusing on capturing towns in the North-east with the ultimate goal of also creating its own Islamic Caliphate. However, this new modus operandi – a departure from the pure hit-and-run guerrilla tactics they are known for – proved difficult to sustain as the method played into the hands the Nigerian military, which still has a reputation as one of the best conventional forces in Africa.

Boko Haram had over-reached, and through July, August and September 2014 it suffered setbacks in the face of an army counter-offensive supported by air strikes. In July Boko Haram took over Damboa, which is about 50 miles southwest of Maiduguri, destroying much of the town and forcing thousands to flee. The military recaptured the city in early August and residents have since begun returning.

In early September 2014 the Nigerian military routed Boko Haram in several battles for the strategic town of Konduga, killing hundreds of insurgents and blocking their path to Maiduguri, the state capital of Borno. Konduga had been the target of multiple attacks owing to its proximity to the state capital, which the Boko Haram had wanted as the capital of their caliphate. In the second attack in the afternoon of September 12, in a convoy of trucks and motorcycles, over 100 Boko Haram gunmen stormed Konduga and hours of fierce fighting with Nigerian military followed. But the Nigerian troops held out against the attack, killing hundreds of insurgents and again blocking their path to Maiduguri.

During the battle the military also claimed to have killed a man who had been impersonating Shekau recent video releases. The death of the "fake Shekau" in Konduga – real name Imam Bashir Mohammed – then immediately prompted questions whether there was another Shekau lookalike ready to continue the fight. However, Konduga, coupled with other strategic military successes appear to have initiated a decisive change of momentum in the conflict.

It was this point in September 2014, that the President of Chad, Idriss Déby, received two letters from representatives of Boko Haram, saying that they wanted to negotiate with the Nigerian Government. "So he [Déby] called Jonathan," Ambassador Tukur said. "And now we are meeting, and the negotiations are still going on."

As a first sign of commitment – and an indication they were talking to the real people – Boko Haram released twenty-seven Cameroonian and Chinese nationals, who had been held hostage for months by the sect. The Chinese workers were seized in May 2014 from a construction camp in Waza near the border with Nigeria. The Cameroonians – including the wife of one of the country's deputy prime ministers – were abducted in July during two simultaneous assaults, also blamed on Boko Haram, in which at least 15 people died. "We were in huts in a pretty dense forest," one of the released Cameroonians, Seiny Boukar Lamine, told state radio.

The release of the hostages – and the fact that the approach had come through Chad – convinced Tukur that he was negotiating with the right people. "Since they delivered on their promise to Cameroon, we expect Boko Haram to deliver on the release of the Chibok girls and the cessation of hostilities in north-eastern Nigeria," he said. "So we declared a cease fire and sat down to talk".

Asked why the talks went through Chad, Ambassador Tukur said: "We were surprised they went via Chad because that is where they get their arms, their arms dealers are Chadians. Initially Chad did not want to cooperate but after the Paris meeting and these discussions with Boko Haram they were now prepared to negotiate. So if Chad was negotiating the Boko Haram knew that their source for arms would eventually dry up. So their best play is to go via Chad and ask to talk to the Nigerians and sit down and discuss."

A further sign of hope was that the military of Chad, Cameroon and Nigeria had agreed to work together and instituted a ceasefire. This is significant because it demonstrated the governments had formally bought into a peace deal. As one intelligence source said: "There was an awareness that the military had to be carried along in any peace deal. If they were not included early on there was no assurance that the peace would hold. The military are essential to monitor and manage the ceasefire. The fact that the military stood down with the announcement of the ceasefire was of enormous importance."

Tukur also explained his optimism: "They've [the Shura Council] assured us they have the girls and they will release them," he said. "We are negotiating with considerable caution. Boko Haram has grown into such an amorphous entity that any splinter group could come up disowning the deal. But we believe we are talking to the right people."

Not unexpectedly, peace did not break out immediately. The announcement of the ceasefire on 17 October 2014 led to a sudden upsurge in Boko Haram attacks and to many people questioning the deal. Another "Shekau" video was released on November 1, which claimed that all of the Chibok schoolgirls had become Muslims. "Don't you know that over 200 Chibok schoolgirls have converted to Islam?" The now slightly fatter and new Shekau said, speaking in Hausa. "They have now memorized two chapters of the Quran. We have married them off. They are in their marital homes."

The most serious incident occurred on October 29 when the insurgents stormed the northeast Nigerian town of Mubi, killing dozens of people and forcing thousands to flee. The insurgents and their heavy firepower, including rocket-propelled grenades, had overrun the commercial hub in Adamawa state. "There is virtually not a single resident left in Mubi. Everybody has left to save their lives," said Habu Saidu, a local resident.

Prior to the attack Mubi had seen an influx of thousands of residents escaping the violence in nearby towns and villages. But according to witnesses the insurgents has now hoisted their black flag over the palace of the traditional ruler, after having robbed banks, burned down the main market and sacked the palace. One described how he saw Boko Haram fighters kill a university lecturer and his entire family. Security fears had already forced the closure of the Adamawa State University, which is based in the town.

Tukur said that in an insurgency in an area like North East Nigeria, communication is hard and there are smaller cells or militant outfits of the group that do not want to give up, even if the core wants to do so. "There are criminal elements within Boko Haram that do not benefit from a ceasefire. They use the insurgency to rob banks, to kidnap, and other activities and so they will not benefit from peace. These vigilante groups will continue to cause mayhem despite the talks, or even to de-stabilise the talks.

"Then there are some hard-core elements, or dissidents, within Boko Haram who thinks they will go to heaven if they continue this 'holy' fight. They won't stop because of the negotiations."

According to another security adviser, "This situation remains caught up in the political game leading up to the elections in February [2015]. To stop Boko Haram you need to cut off the money supply feeding the beast." He then added: "These are very powerful and wealthy people. The sponsors are determined to crush the peace talks and the release of the girls by breaking the ceasefire agreed by Nigeria, Cameroon and Chad. They have threatened commanders that anyone who engages in the peace talks or attempts to handover girls will be killed. To breach the ceasefire they have had some commanders launch attacks on villages and kidnap more girls."

Tukur explained: "People forget that fighting an insurgency takes time. Look at other countries. Normally it takes 20 or 30 years. And even if you solve the big problem, there are still smaller elements to deal with. But we have brought Boko Haram to the negotiations table. Things have turned against them. They have suffered some considerable military defeats and the military has now pushed them out in the Sambisa forest, where even getting food is difficult. Where our military is monitoring them. International eyes are now focussed on the sponsors of Boko haram, and they are suddenly seeing their funding squeezed. So their supply line is being cut, they have the guns but they are now lacking the bullets."

But the battle is far from over. Intelligence analysts who have spent most of their life investigating extremist terrorism agree that the way to counter Boko Haram is to secure the support of the community, obtain reliable and timely intelligence and, most importantly, cut off the money supply. Even the most hardened terrorist needs funds to eat, obtain petrol and buy weapons.

"Boko Haram exists while there is space for it," one analyst said. "Boko Haram needs to be thoroughly understood before it can be effectively countered and dismantled. Only then can an alternative be introduced, targeting the key leadership, isolating the group from media outlets, drawing foot soldiers into alternative employment, and providing corrective teaching through mosques and madrassas. At the same time, they must ensure revenue flow from central government to local communities, enhanced border control, and control of illegal weapons."

These analysts also argued that this must be underpinned by well-equipped security forces who are capable of carrying out clinical counter-terrorism operations. The Jonathan administration has rebuilt the armed forces including establishing a Special Forces brigade. But the Nigerian military is excessively secretive and could do more to gain the trust of the public. One American security analyst remarked that he knew more about the Russian armed forces than he did about the Nigerian military which he classified as one of the most opaque in the world. Secrecy, he said, was a serious threat to the armed forces of Nigeria.

Despite these institutional flaws, the President's envoy Hassan Tukur claims that Jonathan has done much to counter the Boko Haram threat: "When it comes to the insurgency the

President is prepared to do so much more to ensure that this crisis comes to an end. For him anything can still be put on the table. While many negotiations before have hit a brick wall he is prepared to do anything humanly possible to see this through. The President comes from a background where he has worked with the militants in the Niger Delta, so he thinks there can be a solution.

"Nigeria is a country with a big heart. We have a history of insurgency and civil war. But we have learnt the gift of reconciliation, and we can welcome them back. The President has reached out to everyone that think they might be able to help, anyone that has a network and contacts with the militants.

"During this crisis with Boko Haram Africa's most populated country got ebola but we dealt with it. The President said that 'if ebola takes over and terrorism is raging the country is dead and I will not let that happen.' We dealt with ebola, and we are still monitoring very carefully. Now we have to deal with Boko Haram.

"But despite all these problems Nigeria is still moving on. Nigeria became the largest economy in Africa in the midst of this turmoil. Nigeria won't stop. It won't be defeated."

The prospects look promising. Only time will tell.

NOTES

Chapter One

[1] "A Paradise for Maggots: The Story of a Nigerian Anti-Graft Czar", by Wale Adebanwi on the Nuhu Ribadu-era at the Economic and Financial Crimes Commission

[2] Interview conducted by Juliana Taiwo, Abuja, Sunday, May 23, 2010, Nairaland Forum
http://www.nairaland.com/451221/jonathans-untold-story-alamieyeseigha

[3] The Days of the Cabal, By Segun Adeniyi. NVS 9/6/11, Jun 11, 2011 - 9:18:17 AM
http://www.ocnus.net/artman2/publish/Africa_8/The-Days-of-the-Cabal.shtml

[4] "Power, Politics and Death", Olusegun Adeniyi

Chapter Two

[1] http://propagandapress.org/2010/01/10/umaru-yaradua-is-brain-dead-turai-yaradua-in-charge-from-saudi-arabia/

[2] Olojede was also the first African-born winner of the Pulitzer Prize

[3] http://www.premiumtimesng.com/news/144418-farida-waziri-disaster-nigerias-anti-corruption-fight-says-obasanjo.html

[4] http://julianafrancis.blogspot.co.uk/2013/09/ibori-recommended-waziri-for-efcc-job.html

Chapter Three

1   http://www.cfr.org/nigeria/nigeria-dancing-brink/p22833
2   http://allafrica.com/stories/201012170823.html
3   http://www.cgdev.org/doc/shortofthegoal/chap3.pdf
4   http://www.huffingtonpost.com/amb-john-campbell/why-nigerias-north-south-_b_817734.html

Chapter Four

1   http://www.ft.com/cms/s/0/78b805ec-5586-11e1-9d95-00144feabdc0.html#axzz32FT795KK
2   http://www.ft.com/cms/s/0/ee617478-8fc2-11e2-9239-00144feabdc0.html#axzz32N9z8qj8
3   http://www.ft.com/cms/s/0/68e76a74-2440-11e3-a8f7-00144feab7de.html?siteedition=uk#axzz33f5aVemk
4   http://www.imf.org/external/pubs/ft/scr/2013/cr13116.pdf
5   http://www.ft.com/cms/s/0/766eb232-2415-11e2-9509-00144feabdc0.html#axzz33f5aVemk
6   http://www.ft.com/cms/s/0/2f2cea4a-bb15-11e3-948c-00144feabdc0.html#axzz33f5aVemk
7   http://allafrica.com/stories/201404110259.html

Chapter Five

1   http://www.ft.com/intl/cms/s/0/47fcaf92-d037-11e3-af2b-00144feabdc0.html#axzz38KlblZIa

Chapter Six

1   The recommendations followed the Council's review of Mr. Sanusi's response to its report on the audited financial statement of the Central Bank of Nigeria for the year ended December

2012 and other related issues, which it described as unsatisfactory.

2   http://www.bbc.co.uk/news/world-africa-26535530

3   https://www.facebook.com/note.php?note_id=426218763098

4   The Nigerian Freedom of Information Act: Guarantees the right of access to information held by public institutions, irrespective of the form in which it is kept and is applicable to private institutions where they utilize public funds, perform public functions or provide public services; Requires all institutions to proactively disclose basic information about their structure and processes and mandates them to build the capacity of their staff to effectively implement and comply with the provisions of the Act; Provides protection for whistleblowers; Makes adequate provision for the information needs of illiterate and disabled applicants; Recognizes a range of legitimate exemptions and limitations to the public's right to know, but it makes these exemptions subject to a public interest test that, in deserving cases, may override such exemptions; Creates reporting obligations on compliance with the law for all institutions affected by it. These reports are to be provided annually to the Federal Attorney General's office, which will in turn make them available to both the National Assembly and the public; Requires the Federal Attorney General to oversee the effective implementation of the Act and report on execution of this duty to Parliament annually.

5   http://www.premiumtimesng.com/news/151161-jonathan-encourages-corruption-nigeria-speaker-tambuwal-says.html
http://www.thisdaylive.com/articles/tambuwal-jonathans-body-language-encourages-graft/166299/

6   http://www.ft.com/cms/s/0/ceca4c64-3493-11e2-8b86-00144feabdc0.html#axzz336OPx0bb

7   http://www.nytimes.com/2012/01/11/opinion/nigeria-hurtles-into-a-tense-crossroad.html?_r=2&scp=1&sq=Sachs%20NIgeria&st=cse&

8   http://uk.reuters.com/article/2012/09/12/uk-nigeria-okonjoiweala-idUKLNE88B01220120912

Chapter Seven

1   http://www.dailymaverick.co.za/article/2010-09-17-goodluck-jonathan-africas-first-socially-networked-president/#.U1pd6V5hl-N

2   http://newsfeed.time.com/2010/09/16/candidacy-by-facebook-goodluck-jonathan-kicks-off-2011-campaign-in-viral-fashion/

3   http://internetworldstats.com/stats1.htm

4   http://www.bbc.co.uk/news/world-africa-11311779

5   http://edition.cnn.com/2012/01/23/world/africa/goodluck-jonathan-profile/index.html

6   http://worldnews.about.com/od/nigeria/p/Goodluck-Jonathan.htm

7   http://www.theguardian.com/world/2011/jan/13/nigeria-primaries-obama-inspiration

8   Jideonwo is also editor of Y!, which claims to be Nigeria's first youth culture magazine.

9   http://www.premiumtimesng.com/news/157111-boko-haram-nigeria-rolls-soft-approach-counter-terrorism.html

10   http://www.theguardian.com/world/2014/aug/26/ebola-africa-rising-narrative

11   http://saharareporters.com/2014/08/27/ebola-jonathan-receives-un-praise-condemns-stigmatization-nigerians-some-countries

Chapter Nine

1   http://www.conservativehome.com/platform/2014/09/jacob-zenn-the-media-must-not-allow-itself-to-be-used-as-a-mouth

piece-by-terrorists.html

2   http://www.360nobs.com/2014/04/boko-haram-leader-shekau-taunts-president-jonathan-in-new-video-you-are-now-too-small-for-me/

3   http://www.voanews.com/content/is-nigeria-losing-war-against-boko-haram-/1897903.html

4   http://america.aljazeera.com/articles/2014/4/23/boko-harams-rootsinnigerialongpredatethealqaedaera.html

5   http://elombah.com/index.php/reports/breaking-news/9853-boko-haram-militants-have-ties-to-the-govt-azazi-v15-9853

6   http://www.dailytrust.com.ng/sunday/index.php/top-stories/11999-fight-against-terrorism-boko-haram-got-expert-training-azazi

7   http://www.nigeriavillagesquare.com/index.php?option=com_content&view=article&id=23999&Itemid=212&page=1

ACKNOWLEDGEMENTS

All books are a collaboration and this was no exception. This book could not have been written without the exceptional research skills of the tireless Helene Wehtje. She also compiled the photographs and the index. We are also grateful to Antony Goldman, the Nigerian expert and analyst, who cast his eye over the manuscript and provided very useful insights. And we are indebted to Dominic Midgley, the journalist and author, for his expert editing and writing skills. He improved the draft material immeasurably.

INDEX

45, 47-52, 54, 59, 60, 62-65, 69-
71, 75, 79, 82, 85-93, 95, 98,
109, 110, 116, 120, 123, 132,
133, 137-140, 142-150, 153, 154,
155, 157, 158, 159, 161, 166,
168, 169, 178, 181, 186, 187,
189, 190, 193, 194, 196, 197,
198, 207, 208, 210, 211, 212,
213, 214, 217, 219, 223, 224
Kabbah, Ahmed Tejan 183, 184
Kale, Yemi 67
Karim, Kola 114
Katsina-Alu, Chief Justice Aloysius 44
Khan Razia 152
Koroma, Major Johnny Paul 183
bin Laden, Osama 206
Lewis, Peter 57, 78
Liberia 175, 177, 178, 182, 183,
184, 185, 189, 192
Libya 179, 180, 181, 189, 190, 192,
207
Lloyd-Webber, Lord 114
Lukman, Rilwanu 118
Machirori, Fungai 176
Malabu Oil and Gas 135, 136
Mali 189, 190, 191, 206, 207, 218
Mandela, Nelson 180, 181,
Mantashe, Gwede 179
Mark, David 30
Mbeki, Thabo 181,
McLuhan, Marshall 155
Melaye, Hon Dino 148
Merkel, Chancellor Angela 155
Mobil Oil 115
Mohammed, Alhaji Baa Fugu 204
MTN 77, 83
National Electrical Power Authority
(NEPA) 87
National Ptriotic Front of Liberia
(NPFL) 183
National Transitional Council
(NTC) 179
Navarro, David 178

Newton, Thandie 162
Niger 100, 166, 191, 209, 211, 217,
224
Nigeria LNG 125
Nigeria National Petroleum
Corporation (NNPC) 84, 113,
119, 120, 121, 122, 123, 125,
129, 133, 134
Nigerian Railway Corporation 97,
98, 9
NITEL 77
Nnaji, Bart 91, 95, 141
Notore Chemical Industries 125
Nur, Mamman 206, 207
O'Neill, Jim 82
Oando 110, 114, 115, 116, 117
Obama, Michelle 3
Obama, President Barack 140, 153,
154, 155
Obasanjo, Olusegun 15, 18, 21, 24,
26-30, 35, 36, 38, 47, 50, 51, 54,
59- 62, 90, 98, 135, 140, 145,
181, 184-186, 195, 196
Odili, Dr Peter Otunuya 26, 27, 28, 31
Oduah, Stella 100, 140, 141
Ogbia Brotherhood 9
Oghiadomhe, Mike 141
Oil and Mineral Producing Areas
Development Commission 10
Ojukwu, Brigader 53
Okilo, Chief Melford 9, 9
Okocha, Jay Jay 89
Okonjo-Iweala, Ngozi 68, 69, 71,
72, 80, 81, 101, 105, 122, 128,
133, 134, 141
Okonjo, Dr Kamene 127
Olojede, Dele 42
Onudieva, Colonel Mustapha 36, 38,
39, 41, 42, 43
Onwuliri, Professor Viola 179, 180
Orjiako, ABC 11
Otedola, Femi 27
Ouattara, Alassane 187, 188

PREVIOUS BOOKS BY
MARK HOLLINGSWORTH:

The Press and Political Dissent – A Question of
Censorship'

'Blacklist – The Inside Story of Political Vetting'
(with Richard Norton-Taylor)

'The Silent McCarthyism' (with Charles Tremayne)

'MPs for Hire – The Secret World
of Political Lobbying'

'A Bit on the Side – Politicians and Who Pays Them' (with Paul Halloran)

'The Ultimate Spin Doctor –
The Life and Fast Times of Tim Bell

'Defending the Realm – Inside MI5 and the War on Terrorism' (with Nick Fielding)

'Saudi Babylon – Torture, Corruption and Cover-up Inside the House of Saud'

'Thatcher's Fortunes – The Life and Times of Mark Thatcher' (with Paul Halloran)

'Londongrad – From Russia with Cash, the Inside Story of the Oligarchs (with Stewart Lansley)